Also by Dave Hopwood.

Top Stories – 31 parables retold with contemporary comments
Pulp Gospel – 31 bits of the Bible retold with comments
Rebel Yell: 31 Psalms – Psalms, God & Rock'n'Roll
Faith & Film – Movie clips that bring the Bible to life
The Bloke's Bible – Bits of the Bible retold for guys
The Bloke's Bible 2: The Road Trip – More bits retold
Sons of Thunder – A contemporary gospel
No More Heroes – Cain, Solomon & Jacob in a modern
tale of men, women, dads and crime

The Shed

Loosely based on Matthew 4 1-11, Mark 1 12-13, Luke 4 1-13

- - - - - - - - - - -

The man in the shed's CV

Age: 45

Birthday: February 29th

Eyes: Hazel

Hair: Brown/greying

Weight: Needs to lose some

Marital/Family status: Separated, no kids

Career: On the rocks

Education/achievements: 6 O' levels, 3 CSEs, cycling proficiency test, 14 cub scout badges, fake *Jim'll Fixit* Badge awarded by the local cubs for eating a mountain of eggs after watching *Cool Hand Luke*, 100m breaststroke, fourth place in the long jump finals in the County Grammar School athletic championships 1976 (actually joint third but unfairly misplaced)

Distinguishing marks: faint scar on back of left hand from childhood encounter with a hot stove, one or two shallow chicken pox craters, damaged ego from a sack-load of disappointment and frustration

Day 1: Freedom

Suddenly he is a free man, cut loose from the moorings of his job, his family, the last thirty years. He feels the mundane responsibilities of daily life slipping from his shoulders, the pressures that came with being the first born son. He becomes aware of a certain euphoria at the thought of the new start and as he trudges further into the desert and away from the noise of life the old images flicker through his mind. The games and the schooling, the wood and the tools, the bantering with his mother, his dear stubborn mother. He has inherited her strength of character without doubt, along with her courage and initiative. She is now a wiry, keen-eyed woman, grey-haired, tough and wily from the years of bringing up a family under the Romans. Still hopeful for her son, still chewing on those ancient prophecies she was given as a young teenage mother, back in the days when she was nursing him in her nervous, cautious arms. She has never stopped believing, never given up hope and has told him often.

He has inherited nothing from his earthly father. How could he when the bloodline has a fracture in it. But he has learnt well, and considering the nature of the times Joseph has been a good dad. A close father, a man who took time and care about raising his boy and teaching him a trade. He turns his hands now as he walks, squints at them in the glare of the sun. Those callused, scarred features, the calling card of the Nazareth tradesman. He likes his hands, had often lain in bed late at night as a boy, turning them in the half light, imagining what wondrous things he might do with them one day. He used to sit in the street during the day, arc them slightly and imagine the sun cupped between his palms. There are nicks and scratches all over his hands now, but he could still hold the sun if he positioned them right.

He thinks he hears shouts from behind, and his heart falls as he fears the audience from his Jordan baptism has followed him. But he turns and realises the sounds of laughter and shouting are in his head, late echoes from the years when he and his friends wrestled and joked in the Nazareth alleys. He was popular as a boy, never short of playmates and accomplices. Confident and capable. Sometimes reclusive too though, sometimes gripped by those unexpected mood swings. But that was a long time ago now. Now is a new time, and it begins here. With rocks and sand, isolation and hunger.

What he has inherited from his real father will become apparent soon enough, and the hungry days ahead will peel back the layers on all of that. In six weeks the times will change. The people will come. But for now the horizon lies parched and empty, the time and the solitude are his. He kneels, grips a fistful of dust and lets it fall from his fingers. Past days, a past life, past job all slipping away from his grasp.

- - - - - - - - - - -

The cabin is little more than a shed with an outside toilet. And that toilet, let me tell you, is very outside. It couldn't be more outside. I throw my rucksack on the narrow single bed, pull out my black leather Bible and drop into the solitary armchair. The arms of it are scuffed like the fist of a tired boxer, the padding is random and unique, the stumpy peg legs scarred from a million kicks and scrapes. This chair has seen some action. It's about to see some more. With forty days on my hands I've chosen madness. I'm here in this cabin, deep in the grounds of an ancient monastery, stuck out on a wind-blasted moor, to get my mind around Lent. The time when Jesus took off to his own boot camp. He didn't retire to a hut with an outside toilet, he took forty days and nights to wrestle with dark forces in a forsaken wilderness. With an outside toilet it must be said, more outside than mine. I wrestle with the frayed straps of my old rucksack; this bag has seen me through since I was in the third form at grammar school. Or year *whatever* as they call it now. It still carries the faint spidery outline of The Clash logo that I etched on it back in the days when I was young, single, confused and full of acne. I tip it up and strew the meagre contents on the bed. I call it a bed, we'll see about that of course. I've brought a couple of massive jumpers, some old t-shirts, two pairs of jeans, a fat fistful of socks and just enough underwear to have something to put on, turn inside-out and back-to-front whilst I wash the other pair. Oh, and a tiny old hardback book by a little-known writer called Pew Hadovood. It goes by the name *Up The Creek Having Burnt The Paddle* and contains soundbite gems on Jesus's desert period. Other than that I just have a few other thumping good reads - the likes of John Grisham, Don Miller, Nick Page, Tony Parsons, Nick Hornby, Conn Iggulden, Rob Bell, Henri Charrière, Paul Rusesabagina, Nick Baines, Philip Yancey, Jeremy Clarkson, C Day Lewis, John Buchan, Sebastian Faulks, Tom Freemantle, Mike Yaconelli, Robert Goddard and Sam Childers. Just a few. I can carry a good shelf-full because they're on my e-reader. Well yes of course I have my Kindle, I'm intending to fast from technology and the modern world, but I need my Kindle. It's vital – there are three Bibles on it.

I flip on the kettle – it's an off-white electric thing, all stains and chipped plastic. There's also a single metal mug, with a plate, bowl and teaspoon, and a dented caddy of tea bags near an old pint bottle of milk. The milk is sitting in a saucepan of cold water to keep it from going off, though you have to wonder why anyone bothered, with the temperature outside being what it is and there just being a tiny one bar heater in the shed. No sugar in sight. It left town with all the other little luxuries. Ah well, Jesus didn't have sugar in the wilderness. He didn't have anything much, not even 'a cup of cold tea without milk or sugar… or tea', to quote an old piece of comedy genius. I add to this collection my stainless steel coffee pot, an old Bisto gravy tin full of filter coffee and a king-size packet of cornflakes.

Then I flick open the Bible to chapter 4 of Matthew's biography of the son of man. Jesus kicks off his three-year travelling life with a real up and down. It starts well enough - he gets baptised by his fast-talking hippy cousin, who's a sort of cross between Jeremy Clarkson and Ian Paisley without the subtlety or good manners, and is publicly recognised as God's answer to Israel's turbulent problems. However, this is no presidential campaign. Having got on the fame train he promptly gets off again at Wilderness Junction and disappears into his own training camp for forty days. A place where he could be tempted to live a life of success, celebrity and power, and yet would choose weakness, loneliness and humility. Choosing to understand and empathise with Jake Blogs, the troubled man in the street. We can't turn stones to bread. Jesus wouldn't do it either then. I can't fly off a building like superman, so Jesus would stick to walking. Admittedly it was occasionally on water, which was impressive. But he doesn't seem to be chasing the superstar life, he doesn't want the world at *his* feet, he'd rather kneel at the world's feet.

It's a hard act to follow.

I look around the cabin, then steer my gaze out of the window at the wildness out there. Jesus understands this. He knows isolation, he knows what it is to be cut off, as he knows what it's like to be popular. Wish I could turn stones into bread. Or custard tarts maybe. A whole crateful. There are loads of rocks outside. Imagine making custard slices the size of a bowling ball. But nope, that won't be happening to me either. I flip a few pages, the biblical equivalent of fast-forwarding a month or two and I find Jesus surrounded by people hanging on to his every word, clamouring for their own bit of this new king on the block. Fame-isolation-fame. And then more isolation as he tears himself away from time to time, no doubt to stay sane and focused amid the noise. And finally – ultimate isolation on two bits of wood. The crowd wouldn't be eager to follow him up that hill. So then... fame-isolation-fame-isolation-conflict-betrayal-rejection-torture-death-and... but I'm moving too fast. I haven't come to this shed for resurrection. That feel-good ending to feel-good end them all. I've come for the sanity, focus and isolation.

I pour boiling water on the circular tea bag and there's the sound of hissing and fizzing as the water scalds the tea. Jesus didn't have PG Tips and a giant pack of Cornflakes. He ate nothing and became very hungry. There are times when the Bible's simplicity makes an art of understatement. Nowadays we're starving if we miss a Mars Bar between lunch and dinner, or dinner and tea, or brunch and supper or wherever it is your culinary geography has led you. I like strong tea with a good splat of milk. But it makes me feel I'm getting older, the taste buds are fading. Jesus was around thirty when he went into that region of wilderness, if I'd have been him my life's work would have been long over fifteen years ago. That's something. What a young man he was. I mull this as I sup my tea and empty my wallet. Two fivers, a twenty, way too many coppers and three pound coins. Not much, but then I won't be needing much, there's no shop here, no bar, no petrol station to nip into for a Yorkie and a Ginster's pasty.

Evening. Eight o'clock and dark already. No light pollution. With no internet/DVD/TV distractions I go outside wondering if I shouldn't just turn in. Crazy of course because the last time I went to bed around this time I was wearing a woggle and had just got in from cubs. But somehow it doesn't seem to matter here. I came to put life on hold. Forget the pressure of having to live like an adult. Just go to sleep because it's dark. I stand cradling tea in my metal mug. There are so many dents and crevices in it – it feels like holding a hand grenade. I once heard it said that you can't see the Great Wall of China from the moon, but you can see the moon from the Great Wall of China. And from a little snatch of rocky ground here in England. Can anyone out there see me? Staring at the night sky, and there's a whole lot more of it out here than there is in the city, reminds me of those words in that psalm, number eight I think it is. What are they again? 'When I look up at the night sky and see the work of your hands - the moon, the stars, the planets - what are mortals that you should think of us, mere human beings that you should care about us?' What amazes me about those lines is that they never date. Written thousands of years ago they still perfectly match the feelings of being a human, standing outside and staring at the vastness of the universe. That endless canvas splashed with those tiny specks of divine paint. And I'm a speck of divine paint on a speck of divine paint. Perhaps being human never dates. We may come with a bag full of gadgets now, and no longer use stones to bring down giants, but we haven't changed that much.

Those stars once served as a nightly reminder to old Abraham that God was with him, a sort of divine post-it note, not on the fridge but on the dark sky. And something up there guided a few astrologers to a baby in

Bethlehem. Some people saw the stars as deities, ruling and governing. But not the God of the Bible, they were just furniture for him, bits of celestial Lego for shaping messages of comfort and hope.

First night I've not checked Facebook in three years. Think I may need some kind of patch.

Day 2: Fox On The Run

'The painful thing about being a Christian, the galling thing, the gut-wrenching truth, is that it's not really just about self-help. If we only meet together and stuff ourselves full of the good things of God then we just get bloated. Spiritual gas. Not a good idea. When Jesus showed up and started teaching the people of God he didn't pull his punches on this one. All through the Old Testament the prophets and seers had kept jabbing the people to look outwards. Jesus continued the fight. His parables are the story equivalent of a right hook.'
Up The Creek Having Burnt The Paddle by Pew Hadovood

- - - - - - - - - - -

A bleary February morning. A long sleepless night. All kinds of creatures stalk a place like this when the lights are out. Plus the bed is wrought iron and designed for pain more than pleasure. Strong coffee, cold cereal, then off to the monastery to hear one of brother Aidan's talks about an eyeful of logs and specks, a carpenter's parable from Matthew's biography chapter five. As Brother Aidan talks, sounding for all the world like Anthony Hopkins on a bad day, we are all handed small bits of kindling. Wood for our own eyes. At the end of the talk we were invited to drop the sticks in a log basket, evidence of our desire to break free from critical spirits and judgmental attitudes. The sound of wood on wood goes on forever as stick after stick flies into the basket making a little kindling mountain. A hill of hope and forgiveness. Treat others the way you want to be treated, be harsh to them and they'll probably be harsh back to you. We shuffle one after another to throw our sticks together, little grey monks in habits and sandals, a smattering of visitors in hoodies and jeans, bristly men of the road in various guises. One or two stay put in their pews. Maybe they've no one to forgive, or maybe they've done their forgiving. I throw my stick for a woman I've lost. For the carnage of a marriage that became toxic and angry. I throw my stick and the sound it makes lodges like a splinter in my mind. It dislodges other sticks and bounces against the side of the basket. Cracks and creaks, the kind of things that made my marriage shatter.

There's a crooked shelf in my shack. I put my e-reader on it. It looks lonely up there on its own, and makes me wonder whether there'll be much call for shelves in the future. With music, books and films all streaming down towards us via broadband we won't need anywhere to put the likes of Dickens, Shakespeare, Rowling and Hornby. It'll all fit very nicely on our wafer-thin readers and bite-size smart phones, thanks very much. I flick open the leather cover, press a few buttons and find *An Ordinary Man*. Paul Rusesabagina saved the lives of twelve hundred Rwandans during the genocide in his home country in 1994. He was the hotel manager at the Milles de Collines in Kigali when the genocide began in April of that year, and very soon the hotel was jammed full of Tutsis fleeing the slaughter of the killing gangs, known as the Interahamwe: 'Those who fight together'. In his book Paul speaks of his secret – he attempted to make contact with the soft spots inside the hardened murderers who came to slaughter his friends. He sought out the compassion within them and appealed to their better nature using reason, humour and wit. He treated them like humans, not animals. Because he wanted to be treated like a human. An extraordinary achievement when you are sitting opposite a machete-wielding soldier who has fresh blood glistening on his clothes.

Jesus lived under an oppressive regime too. It's easy to forget that. He didn't spend his days in a leafy suburb with the Sunday papers and endless cappuccinos. He lived somewhere more in line with Burma or North Korea today. Injustice woke him up every morning. And here he comes telling people to forgive. To choose to make changes in themselves before demanding this of others. To consider the fact that the speck we see in another's eye is often the reflection of the log in our own. Judging comes easily to me, I don't need an education in it, I don't need to read books or attend courses. I just need to spend time with other flawed human beings. It's that simple. Jesus knows about that, he grew up with other kids, argued with them, bantered, played, joked, won and lost with them.

I make another coffee, a strong one and I take it outside.

I'm feeling hard done by because I've lost a little home comfort. Thinking about oppressive regimes puts it into perspective. Sort of. Because... and I'm not proud of this... I can know about Rwanda and first century Palestine and still be more concerned about my own well-being. I can take self-obsession to Olympic heights. I am the centre of my world. Me, me, me. And if there's a God then surely he is all about making me feel better. Ransomed, healed, restored, forgiven. I want a good life, an easy life, a full life. Full of satisfaction and comfort. Not this cul-de-sac I find myself in. Not this guilt-strewn, regret-laden back alley, full of the garbage of my own mistakes.

There is a mist hanging low like a smattering of dry ice, as if God's pumping it across his stage. I sip my coffee and walk for a while, the steam from my cup adding its own little haze to the fog out there. I come to a dishevelled piece of water, an unkempt lake as if it's on its day off, hasn't dressed properly. Bits of gorse and scrub bushes lie untidily round the edges, and an old wooden bench sheds paint and rots sadly as it crouches at one end. I shuffle over to it. Nurse my drink. Think about sticks in buckets and specks in eyes.

I'm not sure which was easier, getting married or splitting up. Which of course sounds odd. I don't mean easier in the emotional, self-confident, pain-free sense, I mean in the logical reaction to things. We met, fell quickly and heavily, didn't waste time dawdling on the brink of engagement, just went to the cliff and jumped. And it was great for a while. Heady, funny, sexy, romantic. Then it wasn't. Once the sheen of being in love began to fade it all quickly became like this bench. Disintegrating and ugly. We were so different, and I know that sometimes that can be good. Sometimes that can work. Opposites attract. But not us. We were like magnets that repelled. It was confusing, like we'd lost the way, and couldn't find the map back to that place called romance. Then she missed a period, and suddenly things looked good again.

A fox. A young one. I haven't moved for so long that he seems oblivious, totally unaware of me. Just pokes his nose out of the bushes, sniffs around and steps out right in front of me. I watch for a while drinking in the rare sight, the colours, the texture of his fur, the little movements of his eyes. I can see a million pictures of this little guy on the internet, videos all over YouTube, but nothing is like this, nothing beats having a wild animal freely step in front of you. Like those moments when you get your own glimpse of God perhaps. People can tell you about him, draw pictures and make movies. But when you get a shot of God yourself, out in the wild of your own life somewhere. That's something else entirely. I can't help wondering whether this isn't such a moment, after the sticks in the basket and the memories this morning, maybe this is God wanting to put a smile back into things. Crack. Creak. I can still hear those sticks falling in.

Of course, having sat totally still for ten minutes, the moment I try to not move it's all over. A quick flick of an ear, a jerk of his head, and the fox cub is gone. I get up, throw the last of my coffee, wander for a while into the mist humming an old Sweet song about foxes and running. I seem to recall Manfred Mann did one too, but it's that old seventies tune that rattles round my brain now as I walk. And as it's upbeat and reminds me of those old days of being a kid, riding round with my parka hanging off my head, with no worries and all the time and safety to play endlessly in the street, I smile.

Day 3: Tempted

He feels lighter. Baggage-free. Clear-sighted, seeing things so much more lucidly. He has had time to reflect on the whirlwind of the last week. It had been growing for a long time that idea, that elephant in the corner of his workshop. The one that just would not go away. He wouldn't be making tables and restoring houses forever. This was all leading up to something. The stories from his mother, the ideas and visions that kept putting in an appearance in his head. The growing sense that God was close. And then the Jordan encounter. His cousin out there, wild and rebellious, the rumours flying around about him. 'The Messiah's here, he's out in the desert wearing goatskins and eating locusts!' And the people flocked, so Jesus went too. His own cousin, being hailed as the one. But not hailing himself as that, arguing defiantly against it of course. He wasn't ordinary, he was a megaphone for the people. A wake up call. Change is in the air, hope is on the way. So get ready, don't miss it. Like Elijah he bellowed and ranted and soon had a line of interested customers. And that's what Jesus saw that day. John had hijacked the Gentiles' baptism and turned it on its head. Everyone needs it now. Jews and non-Jews. Everyone needs to get in that water for the new Exodus. Cross over to the new land, the land of John and his coming Messiah. So Jesus went in, and the whole thing set off a tsunami of events involving doves and thunder in the sky and John's very public pronouncements about him. So he had been right all along. This was leading somewhere. It had sometimes seemed a long time coming, seemed like a dream, like wishful thinking in a dark night, but now here he is. It has led him to the desert. The moment of fame suddenly passed. Real but gone. Now he's alone. Now he must find himself. Now he must get well-grounded in reality, because there are sure to be many times ahead when others will want him to escape it.

- - - - - - - - - - -

Up early again, make some strong coffee (the milk's starting to turn but this is the wilderness, it's more than Jesus got) and I slump in the battered chair. It's starting to feel like it fits me, always takes a while for me to own a place, but it's beginning to happen here. I read some of Grisham's *The Street Lawyer* for a while. It inspires and disturbs and depresses me. Inspires because it's a great story of a rich man pushing aside his wealth to help the poor. Disturbs because of the tales of the weak and marginalised. Depresses because I am not made of the same kind of stuff as Mr Grisham's lawyer.

Admittedly I'm not filthy rich like the men in John G's world. I have enough to get by for now. It doesn't cost much to stay in a shed in the grounds of an old monastery so my redundancy money is hardly dented. My ego on the other hand is another story. There's nothing like the loss of a good job, nothing like having your earning potential whipped away, for making you feel helpless and impotent. I should be able to wallow in this time. Will one day look back and wonder why I didn't appreciate it more, when I'm dragging myself out of bed for another early start, jumping on a bus to some dead-end job which just about pays the rent, I'll look back and long for these days when I have no pressure, no calls on my time. No boss to please or bills to pay. Did Jesus look back on the simplicity of his days in the desert and wish for that time back? When the crowds were pressing in on him, and the scribes were insulting him and his close friends were trying to push him towards their agendas, did he rue the passing of the time when he was alone and able to set his own plan for the day. The problem for me is simple. I'm still walking out of the shadows, limping away from the work and relationship loss. There's nothing quite like the car wreck of a lost marriage for making you feel something of a loser and an ugly failure. The arguments about blame and the angry flashpoints are still not far beneath the surface. Along with the debilitating lack of desire to believe in something better.

CS Lewis once wrote, 'Remembering is the last chapter'. One day in the future, when I'm sitting under a blanket, flicking back through an e-reader full of memories, I will turn the page on my life and come to this section. I'll glance down the paragraph and recall these days, and there'll be a sweet ache in my heart about the time I was free enough to spend a month in a monastery. When you do these things you often think it'll be easy to do them again some day. But there's no guarantee of that. This is one of those times of my life. I'll appreciate that when it's gone.

I put down Mr Grisham's good book and take up God's. My leather-backed Bible tells me of three temptations Jesus faced in his desert. Bread. Idolatry. Testing God. Moses had made magic bread appear from the heavens, why shouldn't Jesus? Why can't he just turn the stones into manna, the dust into divine flour? If Moses had done this in the desert then it clearly was God's will. It wasn't cheating to feed his hunger like that. Bring it on. Let the soft doughy stuff rain down. Do a Moses. The snag is free bread didn't appear to create a watertight dependence on the breadmaker. I'm not sure if calf became a dirty word in Moses's desert but it certainly provided one of the great joke lines in the Bible. Moses appears with God's brand new 'to do' on a couple of stone post-it notes and all he can say is, 'Where did this Jurassic gold statue come from?' 'Which one?' asks his brother, always a useful playing for time device, 'Oh you mean the one everyone's dancing around as if it's a god? Er... No idea. I just happened to toss a few bellybutton rings into the fire and – hot dang! Out came that creature. Wasn't anything to do with me, guv.' Jump a couple of millennia and here's Jesus being offered the world at his feet, all he needs to do is get his priorities wrong, worship the wrong thing. Bring on another golden calf and some dancing girls. Follow the line of power instead of the way of peace.

And then that strange incident on the temple. In Luke's blog about Jesus it's the last temptation, in Matthew's it's the jam in the middle of the other two. Did Jesus walk and climb up to the top of the temple? I grab my e-reader and scroll to Nick Page's book *The Wrong Messiah*. Apparently Jesus could have walked there in a couple of days, and he clearly had time on his hands. However it happened, vision or visit, when he was up there the whisper in his mind suggested he check that God was really with him. Best do that if you're going to die for everybody and you're trusting in a resurrection moment. Just throw yourself off and see how many angels come running. Won't hurt anybody. Especially not you, as long as the angels turn up. According to

Nick Page there's another spin on this story too. Execution by stoning often involved being thrown down from a great height before being clubbed with rocks. We come across this on one occasion when the crowd push Jesus towards a cliff edge with the threat that they will stone him. There are accounts of blasphemers being thrown down and executed from this point on the temple. The point Jesus is on now, contemplating his own death. Not too long from now Jesus will be accused of blasphemy and taken to a place of execution. And here he is now, pre-empting that. Standing high up, being tempted to throw himself off and not die. To survive. To avoid death by sacrifice at all costs. 'To come down and save yourself,' as the audience said when they were watching Jesus suffer on a Roman cross.

These must have been overpowering experiences for Jesus, especially weakened by the lack of food. Makes me wonder whether I should be fasting? As part of my attempt to identify with the wilderness experience. Not for the forty days but for one day, or half a day, a morning. Well breakfast at least. I glance down at my midriff, it wouldn't do any harm. But that's not the motivation. Of course not. Fasting's not some kind of divine slimming plan. But my motives are already getting mixed. I read Luke's biography chapter four again. The problem is I can't quite see myself in these temptations right now. There are other shadows lurking, other temptations waiting by my door. The seven dwarves of failure. Self-loathing, despair, revenge, depression, anger, regret, and yes, self-gratification to bury the pain. So the magic bread part does fit.

In the film *The Last Temptation* Jesus faces other temptations in the wilderness, the temptation to be with a woman, to give up and save himself, the temptation to have a family, to conquer the world, the temptation to sell out, to eat the fruit that Adam ate. This version of the ordeal Jesus faces is not quite so clear cut as three offers from the devil and three responses from Jesus. And though this is not the biblical account I can't help wondering just how much temptation Jesus faced. Perhaps the testing came at him every one of those forty days, and perhaps it was a lot more devious than we imagine. Perhaps it came at him every day of his life. And did it include my seven dwarves? I can't help hoping so, not to put Jesus through even more agony, but because there's a little saying tucked away in an anonymous letter to a bunch of Hebrews. And it assures me that in Jesus I have a hero who understands my weaknesses because he experienced all the same temptations I experience. Now he may have chosen a different outcome, but I need a soul-mate who's been there. Done that. Stared into the darkness and walked through the tunnel.

I put down my half-empty, ice cold coffee and walk outside. That is the one massive advantage of a shed on the moor. You just step out the door and you're on the wild side. I walk for a bit and I think of the temptations I face. Sex comes to mind, It always comes to mind. Whether or not I'm having much. It's just always there, hanging around in the corner like a sulky kid at a disco. There are too many magazines, adverts, mid-riffs on show. I wonder how I'll cope here, when the boredom and routine starts to set in, when the novelty has worn off and I don't feel so spiritual anymore. Where will my head take me then? I shake it off, literally, shake my head violently, then check to see no one is around to see me behaving madly. There is. It's always the way. Drop your guard for a moment, let out your insane side and there's sure to be witnesses. I grasp the nettle and wander over to them. Two guys watch me approach them. They look serious, earnest, as if they are about to take on the world and win. I steel my nerves and walk right up to them, very un-english. I say 'Hi', they smile. I ask them how it's going. They tell me it's good. Not sure what *it* is yet. They look set for an adventure. Trendy waterproof jackets, trendy rucksacks, trendy waterbottles. All very trendy. Although the shorter guy looks a little ill at ease with all the gear, like it's a sweater his gran knit and it doesn't quite fit him. They tell me they're staying in another cabin in the grounds. They've come to work out what to do next, they say.

'After what?' I ask.
The taller one, the one with the suntan and the carefully-crafted stubble says, 'We're fed up.'
I nod, I know that feeling. The other guy agrees.

'Every Sunday it's the same,' he says, 'we go to church with high hopes and come out feeling desperate and angry. We've had enough.'

'So being here is...' I don't finish the sentence because I'm hoping they will.

'Lots of things,' says the tall guy, 'an escape, time to think, time to plan. To let off steam.'

'What are you planning?'

The short guy laughs. 'We're not sure yet. Maybe start something.'

A revolution? A riot? A new political party?

They both laugh now.

'A church,' they say, and the tall one holds up his hand, 'but don't mishear that. We want to start something where guys can feel at home. You know, they won't have to sing songs which talk about how Jesus is beautiful and they won't have to hold hands or do action songs or listen to sermons full of clichés.'

I nod. I've been there.

'Good luck,' I say, 'if you can do it then...'

'Oh we can do it.' The short guy is suddenly serious. He has a crevice in his chin and a scar by one eye. I don't think I'd mess with him if he told me to come to his new church. 'Yea, we can do it,' he says, 'it's just when and how and where.' They make an odd couple, the short stocky one wouldn't be out of place in a street fight, the taller guy looks more like his manager. Or his bank manager.

I raise a finger. 'What do your families think?' I ask and they both wince.

'Yea, that's the snag,' the tall one says. He jabs a thumb at the short guy. 'His wife doesn't see the problem with church and mine wants to be in charge of anything we start.'

Ah.

'I just want to be able to go to church and not have to pretend all the time,' says the short one, 'I want to speak the way I speak at work.' He punches me in the shoulder. It hurts a little. 'You must know what I mean.'

I resist rubbing the shoulder and nod. 'I do,' I say. 'Only, I don't have any work anymore.'

They looked worried.

'Man that's bad.'

'Oh I have time to look for something. And it means I have the freedom to come here. I've come for a month.'

They look impressed. I feel I've finally scored a point here.

'A month in boot camp,' the short guy says. 'We're only clocking up a fortnight.'

'Yea, well... to be honest I'm grateful for it,' I tell them, 'I wanted to get away for a while.'

'Yea, but those sheds.'

I shrug it off. 'Oh lack of comfort's not a problem,' I lie easily with a smile.

'Hey, we're heading off to find a crag for some free climbing, want to come?'

Another easy lie. 'Oh I'd like to but...' And I adopt the kind of expression that says, 'I need space 'cause I'm working through something right now.'

They nod understandingly.

'I'm Steve by the way,' says the tall one. His handshake would intimidate a bench vice.

'Bill,' says the shorter guy, and I don't take his hand. We just nod in each other's general direction.

'Well, we'd better go,' says Steve, 'lots of climbing, you know. See you around,' and they trudge off.

I stand, watching them walk away, and I realise what a mess I feel. On the one hand I know exactly what they're talking about. I can't stand church either. I don't like all the Christianese and the shiny idealistic happy songs. And I lay all that at the doorstep of wanting something more manly. But then I get invited to go climb a mountain, or kick a football or shoot a clay pigeon and I crumble inside and feel a sham. Not a man at all. Not a woman either. Not anything really. I just can't seem to do the blokey thing. And I'm not sure what the alternative is.

Meeting those guys has made me realise something. I'm not angry anymore. At least not about church. I used to be, I used to come out of Sunday services and stomp around like Jesus wrecking the temple. Only I wasn't annoyed about righteous things like justice, freedom, or equality, I used to swear at the sky and yell about the action songs, or having to hold hands with the guy next to me. Or the total irrelevance of it all. I don't know when I stopped stomping but at some point I did. At some point I yelled my last time, shook my fist and my head in one final deflated gesture. Now there's a towel lying on the floor of the ring, I know 'cause I'm the one who threw it in. The machine is too powerful. The problem too deep. The ingrained way of doing things too complex. Church is a way of life and you can't come along and get apoplectic about it every Sunday. You'll have a heart attack. No. I don't get mad about church anymore.

There are too many faithful people who have dedicated their lives to the cause, given themselves wholeheartedly to the way church is... I understand that now... I see that. I see that someone like me coming along with my contemporary ideas and blokey attitudes just unsettles them. Better to settle for extra-curricular activities for us guys, drinks in the pub, curry nights, movie evenings, cooked breakfasts with a speaker from the local football club or science lab. Best just to grin and bear it when it comes to Sunday. No good lighting a stick of dynamite and putting it under the vicar's cassock. Won't do at all. Just end up with blood on the vestry carpet.

Steve and Bill shrink down to a dot on the horizon. They're determined. They won't just get mad, they'll get even. They'll start a revolution, light a fire that no one can put out. They'll climb a whole load of hills and plot their big plan while they do it. Me, I'll just nip off to my shed and make a few notes with a cup of coffee.

Jesus was a carpenter of course, I chew on this as I amble back. He was probably a builder too and we all know how blokey they can be. And not just a builder, he was a massive great chunk of rock. A solid cornerstone that could take the weight of the world. I guess Jesus was at ease with his manhood. I doubt he would have been threatened by Sharp Steve and Bill Blunt. So... can he understand someone like me? Someone who is easily threatened? Someone who isn't a reliable piece of granite? Someone who feels more like playdough? Does he get that?

I shake my head and wander back to my shed. I feel like getting under the covers and staying there for a long time.

Day 4: You Think That I'm Strong

'The wilderness can be heaven or hell, sometimes a tortuous mixture of both. But anyone making the tough choice to follow a guy calling himself the son of man will surely find themselves in one sooner or later. This Christianity lark is no crutch, no easy option, no piece of cake. It's been known to get people killed.'
Up The Creek Having Burnt The Paddle by Pew Hadovood

- - - - - - - - - - -

Brother Basil has his own cottage on the estate. He's the longest serving member of the monastery, keeps chickens and his garden looks like Steptoe and Son took over running Eden. I fight my way through it as I attempt to find his front door. Bits of ancient tractors protrude from clumps of rhododendrons and stinging nettles. Here and there I see bits of Noah's ark lying about, there's a port hole off the Titanic over there, and a corner of The Ark of the Covenant juts out from under a mound of mud, chicken dung and dead grass.

For some reason I'm scared, as I meander up the short path from the rusty iron gate, skewed off its hinges, I feel my heart racing. Crazy. I'm going to meet an old monk, twice my age and half my weight and I'm terrified. Something in me fears that the wisdom of age could be a lethal weapon. That he'll somehow be able to 'see' things in me. The pain from the divorce, the regret over the baby, the anger over my job loss, the ancient malingering guilt from those wild days of youth. Anything really, anything that I fear others seeing, he may be able to spot. The embarrassments especially. There is a saying they use in therapy. 'Wherever you go, there you are.' In other words you can run, but you can't hide... from yourself. Because you go with you wherever you go. Spain. The closet. The toilet. Marriage. Divorce. Parenthood. Vegas. Success. Failure. Venus. Mars. The wilderness. A cabin in a monastery. Even Brother Basil's study.

Wherever you go you take yourself with you.

Brother B greets me at the door as if I'm his long-lost schoolmate. His eyes shine and his crooked mouth beams at me. I've never met him before, we've just been assigned to each other, him to sort me out, me to be terrified of him. He grips my right hand between both his and literally pulls me inside with a charming kind of glee.

'I've been so looking forward to meeting you,' he chortles, still grinning.

For some reason I think of those spiders who devour their unsuspecting victims. Brother B is more like an oversized teddy bear, a little scruffy and threadbare, round in the middle, but in no shape to eat me really.

He takes me into his study. I have never seen so many books, so many old books, so many huge hardbacked books. They are on shelves everywhere, and two saggy armchairs and a tiny coffee table sit amongst the literary debris. He gestures happily to one and plonks himself down in the other. He has at last let go of my hand.

'I'm scared,' I say, which is not like me at all. Never admit the truth, that just leaves you wide open to ridicule and criticism. Why am I telling this manically happy monk such a naked admission?

He laughs.

'I think we all are,' he says. 'A whisky?'

My eyes burst wide like a couple of exploding fireworks. He giggles.

'Actually, it's a bit early isn't it? Tell you what, come back later one evening and we'll open a bottle then. You do like whisky?'

I did.

'Goodie,' he says. 'We'll do that then. Now,' he places his fingertips together and presses them to his old lips. 'You're quite unusual.'

'Am I?'

'Yes, we don't often get men coming here for a whole month. Especially not young men. Have you nothing better to do? Chase women or watch football?'

For a moment I am thrown again. Nothing better? But surely coming to a monastery to be with God...

He laughs.

'I'm teasing you,' he says. 'I'm just surprised. Are you... between jobs perhaps?'

I nod. I am between everything.

'Really? Your life is as they say – on hold?'

It is. Why does that suddenly sound feeble? There are days when it seems like an adventure, the freedom to start over, but not right now, not sat in Brother Basil's overcrowded study. Not here with this old monk who chats about whisky and chasing women.

'Men are very afraid aren't they?' he says, as if reading my thoughts. 'And Christian men can be especially so. It's so counter-cultural isn't it? Admitting you need God, admitting you muddle up on a regular basis. Facing yourself and dealing with your demons. It's not as manly as go-karting and drinking beer is it?'

I laugh now. 'No,' I say, 'it isn't.'

'I've only been go-karting once,' he says, 'I rather liked it but I kept bashing my knees when I cornered, these old habits don't provide a lot of padding you see.'

I do see, though I can't quite imagine him squeezing into a go-kart wearing his monk outfit somehow. Presumably the brothers all went on some kind of a communal retreat day, held on a race track at breakneck speed.

'I went to a big Pentecostal meeting a while back,' he says, his fingers still pressed together, 'I'm not a big singer, I often mime the plainsong we use here. So I just sat and happily watched and listened. It was quite fascinating. And I did rather think there was a kind of fervour born out of the desire to avoid the fear and uncertainties. You know what I mean? If we just pray and sing a bit louder we can drown out the sorrows, that sort of thing. Please don't think I'm being critical, it just left me wondering about our need to run away from the doubts and fears and misgivings.'

'But aren't you afraid at times?' I ask him.

'Oh yes, of course, most of the time, that's why I became a monk! But I'm not afraid of being afraid. I think I'm starting to realise it's part of being human. And being English! We're so embarrassed a lot of the time, aren't we? When we meet people, when we say goodbye to them. When we talk about the weather and all the bad news. When we meet friends in the street, or when our dogs and our children force us to meet strangers. Embarrassment floods our veins really doesn't it? I could be wrong of course. I think I was wrong once…'

For a moment he looks off into the distance as if trying his best to recall that strange and singular moment, then his eyes flick back to mine and his wry smile turns into a huge grin.

'I do waffle on don't I?' he said. 'You're supposed to be telling me about you.'

So I tell him. Some of it. But not all, because I am too scared and embarrassed. I say more than I intend though.

'And then she had the miscarriage, and that seemed to pull the rug again. The promise of the baby had kind of been the glue that had held us together, more than that I suppose, it had drawn us back together. But then we lost the glue… sorry, I don't mean that, it wasn't glue it was a baby…'

And then I do the most unmanly thing possible. I start to cry. I don't know why, I didn't see it coming. There's been no warning so that I can change the subject or pretend I have something in my eye or feign a coughing fit. I just sit there and sniff a lot and can't stifle the tears. And when I steal a glance at Brother Basil he is crying too. I don't say much after that, I can't. We both sniff and snort for a while and then I stand up.

'I'm sorry. You were right, I'm not much of a proper man at all,' I say, sorting out my eyes with the back of my fist.

He frowns. 'No,' he says, 'not so much a 'proper' man, more a human being, and when you become more human, you become a little more godly you know.'

Brother Basil smiles.

'Come back soon,' he says, 'we'll have that whisky.'

I nod and sigh and let myself out.

Day 5: (I can't get no) Satisfaction

There's no one there. He thought he heard a voice but there is no one there. He grabs his sandals, pulls them on. Fixes the leather. Is he going mad? Was it his own voice? Is he talking to himself without even realising it now? He walks again. He will go to the temple soon. Something inside of him is urging him to go. He brushes sand from his face. He didn't sleep well, his head is thick with the morning heat and the lack of rest. A figure flashes by him. He turns quickly. An angel? A lion? An apparition? Nothing. There is no one there. No sound of pounding feet. He walks on. He does what he did yesterday, tells himself stories. He's taken to doing this, regurgitating the tales he grew up with, retelling the past. Good rabbis tell the best stories. Tales of the unexpected, tales that turn people towards the kingdom, tales that irritate like sand in a shell, niggling away until the pearl emerges. So far he has come up with one about a widow and a judge, one about a seed sower and two about fathers and sons. He dreamt in his fleeting moments last night about the wise woman from the book of proverbs, he can see her now, wild hair and eyes gleaming, dressed for her party and out in the street yelling at the passers-by. Goading the wise and the stupid to come home with her where she has a table stacked with wine and food for them. 'Come to the party,' she says, 'learn and grow and celebrate.' That's today's story, he decides, only it won't be about a wild woman, it'll be about a king, and he'll invite the wise and the stupid and they won't come. They'll make excuses instead. And if they do that – who else can the king invite?

- - - - - - - - - - -

It's amazing how quickly some welcome time out can turn to isolation... and then isolation to loneliness. And I'm only five days in. I think it's the realisation that I don't have a choice. The small and tough Mother Theresa once said that loneliness is like an epidemic in the West. It is in this cabin right now. The walls seem closer than ever, the stones outside a lot less like bread or custard tarts. If I could turn them into gerbils right now I would, hamsters, voles, velociraptors, any other living creature to give me some distraction. I turn to Luke's biography of Jesus, chapter three, there's a list there of Jesus's ancestors, a kind of 'Who does thou thinkest thou art?' kind of thing. Luke seems to be making the point that Jesus is real flesh and blood, with a startling back catalogue of a dysfunctional family. He's not Clark Kent just waiting for the next phone booth to come along. All his superpowers are in storage. I wonder how lonely he got out there? Did he end up talking to the rocks and tumbleweed for a bit of company. I'm talking to myself all the time. I'm doing it now. It's lunch time, a good excuse to escape the solitude and go and sit with others in silence.

The food here is okay, I tell myself in another happy monologue as I walk along to the refectory, it's simple and basic and repetitive, but then it's designed to be. It's for monks dedicated to a life of poverty and men of the road who happily welcome the chance to slurp hot chunky soup and paving slabs of brown bread, slathered in marmite thick enough to ice a cake. I don't need fast food and chocolate. I don't need curry and roast beef and Yorkshire pudding. I'll kill for it right now but I don't need it. I'd go to prison for a full English, which of course would defeat the object as I'd then be on prison food.

The soup today is cauliflower. Better than pea. Thick pea soup nearly killed me yesterday. If Wednesday is always pea remind me to turn up late in time for the brown bread and marmite course. Brother Aidan reads to us as we eat from something called *The Beautiful Manifestations of the Mysterious Cloud of Knowledge* by an old Saint from the 14th Century. I don't understand too much of it, and it seems to repeat itself an awful lot, but there is something about the presence of those words, written in faith and humility, that gets to me. This message from six hundred years back, still being read to the faithful and doubters today. As I sit there I realise I begin to eat in rhythm, the spoon moving up and down from the bowl in time to Aidan's gentle metre.

The process gives me time to reflect on yesterday's meeting with Brother Basil, I've held it at arm's length, embarrassed by the emotion of it, but now as I chew on it the memory seems a good one. Brother B didn't say as much as I thought he might, and he didn't ask many questions at all, yet somehow I feel I've come out of it a little different. Like going through a car wash. Although I guess walking through one of those would smack you about as much as spruce you up.

Being here in the big house with this ragtag collection of monks, visitors and vagrants the intensity I felt earlier fades for a while. I glance around and some of the visitors smile back at me. It's strange for them too. We are all adjusting to this non-tech world where the rhythms of life are on a constant slow, where the days move along like a steamroller with the handbrake on. We all chose it, we all liked the idea when we thought of it in our high-tech stressful places back home. But acclimatising to this pace is another story, we need something to help us come off the drug of modern life. And all we have is Brother Aidan, cauliflower soup and a repetitive saint from the Middle Ages.

Brother Aidan looks fierce to me. And a hundred years old. He has a creased face and looks like Mick Jagger with a severe haircut. I imagine him suddenly breaking out with *Hey you! Get off of my cloud* or *Jumping Jack Flash it's a gas-gas-gas*. If he said it in the same rhythmic, gentle patterns we'd probably not notice. I keep glancing shyly at him, fascinated by the way his thin lips go at the words in front of him. He's raised up a little, in a kind of pulpit embedded in the wall. It probably has a few buttons inside and when pressed in the right order the pulpit almost certainly rises up and disappears through the ceiling. I wonder how a man like that becomes a monk, or indeed any man, whether they resemble the lead singer of The Rolling Stones or not.

I'm still wondering when a bell rings and everyone stands, chairs scrape, some of us cough, and Brother Aidan closes his book. He says a blessing in Latin and we slip away.

I meet Tosh in the quad outside the refectory. A small square of ground, all flagstones, grass and ragged hanging baskets. He's sitting on a bench and I drop down next to him. Then I regret it. He doesn't smell good. The monastery has its fair share of homeless visitors who drop by, men of the road who find a smile and a bowl of soup. It doesn't take long for me to decide I've made a mistake. Tosh may not bath much but boy can he talk.

He knows his Bible too. Quotes it right, left and centre. For a long time he tells me about the book of Daniel and how it's all coming true right now as we sit there on that bench. Then he monologues on the government, the health service, education, the British Empire, Bruce Forsyth, Beyoncé and the shipping forecast. He leaps from one subject to another seamlessly, obviously well-versed in the art of rambling randomness. He'd do well on *Just a minute*.

Part of me, most of me wants to get up as soon as possible. There's barely an ounce of me that wants to stay and hear this out.

Eventually I get a word in edgeways, but only to ask him how he got here. He knows what I mean, I'm not talking about his mode of transport to the monastery.

'I was going to be a priest,' he says. 'But I fell in love and then my wife got pregnant and so I got a job, we bought a flat. It was all okay for a while and then I started drinking, I don't know why, boredom maybe. Frustration too. Disappointment that I couldn't be a priest anymore. Lost my way. We started to argue and my work began to suffer. It was hard being a father with a young baby in a small flat.' He shakes his head. 'It's all so unremarkable isn't it? Just like that song, what is it? You know, that one by the band Squeeze.' He snaps his fingers a few times. '*Up the Junction*.' He laughs. 'That's the one. *Up the Junction*. I never thought it would happen with me and the girl from Clapham... Well she wasn't from Clapham but it went pretty much the same way. We both got fed up with me. She moved out, I drank more, lost my job. Couldn't pay the mortgage. Lost the flat. She didn't want to have anything to do with me. I stayed with friends for a while but they all got tired of me. I was an embarrassment and I was unreliable. Came home all hours. Tried a few jobs but just didn't seem to have the staying power. Eventually ended up where I am now. Travelling. Sleeping rough. Coming here when I can. Funny thing though. Gave up the booze.'

He grinned at me and nodded. Stopped talking for the first time in ages.

'Grew up normal you know,' he said suddenly. 'Thought I might be a pilot when I was a kid. Loved those Airfix model planes. Used to make them all the time. Paint them the right colours. Stick the markings on the wings.'

He makes movements with one hand as if he is holding one of his models, swooping and diving like a Spitfire chasing a Messerschmitt, I half expect him to make the noise of gunfire, the boyish 'Rat-a-tat-tat!' but he doesn't. He just drops his hand to rest in his lap.

'I remember coming home one day. Frustrated about something. Took one of those planes and smashed it against my bedroom wall, again and again and again. Then I painstakingly collected all the pieces, glued it all back together and fixed it up again. Never became a priest or a pilot though. Dreams. Just wild dreams. Smashed up. Smashed up so bad. That little plane. A Hurricane I think it was. Gone now. All gone.'

He sighs, gets up and walks away. Then he stops and looks back. 'Thanks for chatting. You're the first person in ages who's willingly sat down beside me.'

Another grin and he ambles off. A few words at the end there, but they turn everything round. Like getting to the end of the book and solving an unexpected mystery or discovering a great secret which affects everything else you've just read. Like the detective was the murderer all the time, that sort of thing. Tosh's thanks and smile make my day. Somehow against my will I did something useful. I know already that this will be the highlight of today, something I'll remember from my wilderness trip.

Day 6: (My Name Is) Michael Caine

'Jesus is a past master at impressions. He can and does do them at the drop of a hat. Elijah, Elisha, Moses, Noah, Daniel, Isaiah, he does them all. His impressions are his qualifications. If he is to be taken seriously as the next man of God then he must look like the old men of God. This is not just about being a good leader or teacher, this is something else. And it's nothing new. Joshua needed a miracle to impress the people after Moses handed the baton to him. So he did what Moses had done, he split water in two. Well, this is the new Joshua, impersonating the old Joshua, impersonating the old Moses, in order to gain respect and show authority. He brings commandments on a hill, he controls water, he crosses a wilderness and he does miracles. All so the people will get divine déjà vu and start to see the bigger picture here.'
Up The Creek Having Burnt The Paddle by Pew Hadovood

- - - - - - - - - - -

Jesus wakes and stretches and rubs the sleep from his eyes. His mouth is dry and he wanders to the nearest stream, not much more than a wet trickle. He leans, scoops, sips and straightens. Then he bends again and splashes his face. He wonders if they'll make the connections. If they'll ever know, and if they know, if they'll get it. Forty days. Like Noah on his boat. Forty years. Echoes of Moses in his desert. Forty. It's no accident. No random figure. He will stay here and face himself, make friends with this tough place. Turn it into home. And if he can do that he knows it will always be there for him. Always be a familiar place, inhospitable and friendly. A place to call his own. When the madness threatens to take hold. When the people clamour once too often. When the pressure to be a superman is too much. Or when he tires of his friends and the misunderstandings and manipulations. He will come here, or to another place just like it. And he will be safe, safe amongst the wild animals and the harsh conditions. Safe knowing that he will always meet God here. And there's no safer place as far as he can see.

His cousin got it. He made the connection. Jesus saw that light bulb moment happen in the water that day. John hadn't known, not at first. Not for a long time. When they were growing up, playing together as boys, hanging out as teenagers, sitting by the road watching the Romans kick up dust, posturing on their horses as they turned up yet again to collect taxes. John had no idea back then. But in those days Jesus was on a voyage of discovery himself. Getting glimpses. Like waking from a dream that you half-remember and when you try and tell someone about it the details become ever more elusive. But that Jordan day, that day not so long ago when Jesus pushed his way through the crowd and they embraced and swapped the usual greetings. Then John had abruptly seen what others couldn't. He had sensed that his cousin was more than a carpenter. God's spirit was on him and John was the man to announce it. A witness, his ultimate purpose. To signify the arrival of God's man. John hadn't known it until that moment, hadn't realised it would be his own cousin, but then suddenly, as they embraced, John had pulled back, his eyes wide. Was it terror or amazement? Hard to tell. Probably both.

- - - - - - - - - - -

It's a beautiful spring day. 2.00pm. Doesn't feel much like a desert at all. Stray daffodils are starting to emerge. Forgotten from last year but still there all the same. Having slept all winter they now crawl back from the dead. Resurrected by the warmth and the time of year. It's one of those days when you feel the warmth on your face as you squint into the sun and remember what good weather is like. The winter is starting to pass. I have my rucksack and a water bottle and the intention to explore. And as I travel I think. And talk to myself.

I've come to the conclusion that Jesus made friends with the desert. When his cousin John was murdered and he got the news the first thing he did was run to the wilderness. Took his grief and his pain and went to the place where he knew he could be himself. And he took his fears too. This is like a premonition for him, the shadow that must fall across his path. John's death is a sign. Walk this way, this road that began for both of them in the wilderness. For Jesus this is the journey that kicked in the day he refused to throw himself off the temple heights and demand that angels catch him. He's going to fall like John to his death. He is going to take his seat on a cross, where the rough wood and razor splinters will dig deep, along with the fists of Rome's hired men and the thorns of a hastily assembled crown.

John is dead. John is dead. His poor cousin. The boy who was once so strong. The boy who began what Jesus must finish. That voice in the wilderness... where did those days go? To John the wilderness was life. Those days he spent ear-bashing the self-righteous and wooing tax collectors, prostitutes, soldiers and Samaritans. Those days when he dragged forgiveness from the hands of the rich powerbrokers and gave it back to the street-people. God is yours. God is here. God is with you! The poor, the sick, the grieving, the rejected, the losers, the wasters, the unloved and unlovely. The unacceptable and those who look cursed. God is with you. Here in the wilderness of life. And now he is gone. John is gone. He was no fragile reed but still he has been torn from the hard ground. The voice will call out no more.

And when he got the news in some strange way Jesus must have felt immediately alone. Though the cousins had drifted apart they had still been on the same mission. Just the two of them bent on this course of destruction and salvation. Jesus had continued the baptising that John began, continued the work of taking forgiveness and hope to the gutters. Continued inviting those on the fringes of life and the edge of acceptability.

John had lost the plot a little towards the end, wondered about Jesus for a while. Maybe prison stole his perspective. Maybe the rumours about Jesus were confusing. The ex-carpenter didn't look much like the man who would separate the chaff from the grain. Sort the dross from the good stuff. He didn't seem to be doing much cleaning up the neighbourhood. Digging out the corruption and expelling the evil perpetrators. It didn't look very much as if the king was bringing in the kingdom. Not the way John expected anyway.

So he had sent friends to confront his cousin. 'What's going on?' they asked. 'Did John get it wrong? Has John failed in his mission?' And Jesus, saddened by the question but inspired to help his cousin in his dying days, replied, 'Look around! The blind see, the poor are lifted up, the dead are coming back to life. Blessed are those who are not disappointed with the way I work. Happy are those who do not give up when I fail their expectations.' The friends of the baptiser looked around, frowned and took the news back to John. Did it lift his spirits? Did he have one final light bulb moment? Jesus hopes so. 'He was a shining light,' Jesus says to the religious leaders around him, 'and you were happy to bask in that light and celebrate for a while. You got the benefit. But the son of man is here now, and he will go the same way as John. In spite of John's testimony about him, in spite of the miracles and the stories he tells. The light is here, but soon it will be extinguished and night will come.'

I wonder whether the sunshine isn't a metaphor for the glory of God. As I stand there and feel its growing warmth I can't help putting the two together. I'm in a small moorland valley and the place is bright and alive with shades and colours. There's a man sitting there on a rock. Can't see who it is. I intend to just walk past him. It's Tosh. I definitely intend to walk past him.

'Hya,' he says.

I nod, still walking.

'Not a bad old day eh?' he says.

I nod and smile, still walking.

'Where you going?'

I shrug. 'Just walking,' I say, still walking.

'I'm dying,' says Tosh and I stop.

'Seriously?'

'Would you take more notice of me if I was?'

An unanswerable question.

'We're all dying,' he says, 'though we kid ourselves not. Being on the road you see it. Sick people everywhere, hellbent on destruction. The road sharpens your perception you know. Especially if you're not on the booze. Cuts through all the bull. D'you believe in Jesus, mate?'

'Of course,' I say.

'There's no "of course" about it. Plenty of non-believers hang around this place. It's comfort. Don't need to believe to find some of that. I saw him once you know.'

'Who?'

'Jesus. Right near one of those cabins. He was standing smiling. You don't see enough pictures of Jesus smiling, people think he's so blooming miserable. Like he's got indigestion all the time. He's not like that. I saw him. I told you, by that cabin. He was totally alive, light shining out of him, better than this sunlight. Wish people could see that. Wish all those po-faced religious types could see it, and all those earnest atheists. And them people with no hope. Jesus has had a bad press. Too many hard-luck stories over the years. He's not what people think. He's not what you think.'

And without waiting for a further answer Tosh straightened, stretched, burped and ambled off.

'See you round,' he calls without looking back.

I nod but he can't see me.

Which cabin? Which cabin was Jesus outside? And when? Has he been there watching me? Is he outside my shed?

Day 7: Travelling Man

Rocks. Everywhere. All shapes and sizes and every one of them could be bread. He licks his lips, his mouth is dry. He reaches for his water-skin. Wets his mouth and swills it around. Splashes his face too. Bread. Everywhere. He knows he could do it. He knows that it's possible to produce bread from stones. He knows that rocks will praise God if the conditions are right. But no one's praising now. It's just him and the dry ground. Rocks. Bread. Everywhere. Everywhere. His stomach groans. Really groans. He walks on but the trouble is you can't leave rocks behind you in the wilderness, they go with you. They don't travel, they just line the way, turn out to greet your every step. He walks on. Rocks. Bread. Manna. His footsteps crunch the words at him. Bread from above. Bread by another name. What is it? Exactly. What is it? He's not the first of his kind to trudge across a desert and hunger for bread. If his ancestors could have magic bread, why not him? Why can't he have a few slices of *What is it?* He recounts the story in his mind. God humbles his people, letting them go hungry then feeding them himself. People don't live by bread, they live by the breadmaker. Without the sun and the rain and the fertile ground, nothing will grow. Bread will not spring from the ground or the sky. He walks on. Moses took seventy men up a mountain and God fed them. He wonders if he might do that. Take some people up a mountain and feed them, and if he does, will they make the connection? One day he'll make bread and some will see that he's the bread man. He was after all born in Bethlehem, *The House of Bread.* The bread of life born in a bakery. There's poetry in that. Bread. Moses did it, he should do it. No. Man does not survive on bread. He needs the breadmaker. No bread. Just rocks. No bread. Just rocks. No bread. Just rocks… just rocks… just rocks…

- - - - - - - - - -

I've decided to break bread every day. Well, not so much bread as biscuit. A Bourbon and a cup of tea around ten each morning. Which of course sounds remarkably like elevenses. But then a sip of wine and a chunk of bread doesn't sound like much till you use it to remember

Jesus. I wake early so 10.30 is well into the day here. I could take communion with the brothers if I wanted, but I'm kind of tired of that at the moment. I need to rediscover the gift of food to remind me of God. Some people might see a cuppa and a cookie as sacrilegious, others might just view it as an early tea-break. But it's not to me. It's a reminder that I need food and drink and I need Jesus. Got to have him. Can't live without him.

Jesus refused to make bread on a couple of occasions. Once on his own and once with a crowd. He wouldn't make magic bread to prove a point. Bread represented compassion to him, food for the hungry, spiritually and physically. I raise my metal cup and turn to John's biblical blog and read about loaves and fishes. There's a knock at the door. I open it. Standing outside in the rain is a guy with dreadlocks and a bike. The bike has the biggest panniers in the world.

'Hi, I'm Stew,' he says, offering his hand. 'Are you a monk?'
I tell him I'm not but I let him in anyway and break biscuits with him. I tell him it's my way of doing communion and he grins.

'Cool,' he says. 'I'm an atheist myself but I can always break biscuits with a friendly limey.'
Turns out he's Australian and he's been cycling the globe for five years.

'Yea, I stop off in places when I need to. Ya know, work in factories or vineyards or cinemas, anywhere to make a few bucks for the next leg of the journey. This is my European phase.'

'You've been on the road five years?'

'Yup.'

'And you're an atheist who's come to a monastery?'

'Yup.'

'On a search for enlightenment?'

'Nope. Need a cheap bed.' And he grins again. He has some of my tea in his own Russell Crowe tin mug.
I ask him how he's finding atheism.

'Well, it's liberating. I can listen to people, learn stuff, don't have to worry about whether it fits with my belief system, I was raised a catholic see, so had to be on my guard about getting contaminated by other people's ideas. The tough side though,' he pauses and stares into his mug, there is silence for a moment, we hear the rain dripping off the gutters outside, 'the tough side is the loneliness. When I'm on my own sometimes I'm really on my own. Know what I mean?'

I shrugged. 'To be honest no,' I said, 'the key thing about my faith is that I'm not my own, with all my mess and my muddling along, I believe he's always with me.'

He nods. I guess he's heard all that before.

'I miss that,' he says with a frown. Then he grins. 'But I get more girls now.'

He pulls out a tobacco tin and some Rizla papers.

'Just gonna roll me a smoke,' he says and he indicates the door. 'Wanna come outside and try and convert me?'

I consider this. The rain is still a steady stream. But I come over all Francis of Assisi.

'Why not?' I say.

We try and shelter in the doorway but even though he's as skinny as a rake neither of us gets much protection from the weather.

'So? What you doing here?' he asks, blowing smoke out of the corner of his mouth.

'Time out,' I say. 'Marriage, job, future… everything's on hold. Plus I wanted to chew on the story of Jesus in the wilderness. You know – the forty days?'

'D'you think he really did that?'

I nod. 'Why not?'

'D'you think he really did all that Bible stuff?'

I nod again. 'Yea. Well, not all of it. He was only on earth for the four gospel biographies. But if it wasn't true why else would a bunch of frightened men living in an oppressed country suddenly decide to risk everything for it?'

'What do you mean?'

'His mates. His disciples. When he died they were scared out of their heads. They were seriously terrified. Running, hiding, pretending they didn't know Jesus. But something changed all that. They ended up going all over the world and dying for what they believed. In fact you and me both know what we know about Jesus because of those guys, if we had records we could trace it all back. Someone told someone who

told someone who told someone etc. and eventually it came all the way from the first disciples to the two of us stood here now in the rain.'
He grimaces. 'Never thought of it that way,' then he grins again, he has a gap between his front teeth which shows when he does it. 'Hey – I bet I go all the way back to doubting Thomas,' he says.
I laugh. 'That's what I always say,' I tell him. 'Maybe we're like – spiritual cousins!'
He smokes in silence for a while. Then, 'Met any good monks?'
      'Brother Basil,' I say immediately, 'but be careful - he can see right through you. Oh and Brother Aidan – you can't miss him. Looks like Mick Jagger, sounds like Hannibal Lecter.'
Stew nods and starts to walk back to his bike.
      'I'll check 'em out,' he says, 'thanks for the bread and wine.'
Bread and wine?
He gives me that grin again. 'Ya know, the tea and biscuits.'
And he saddles up and rides off, standing upright on the peddles as he goes.

When I talk to Stew I sound so confident, so full of faith. Like I'm St Paul or someone. He should see me at 3am sometimes. When I wake up in the dark and wonder what on earth it's all about.

Day 8: The Fame Monster

'Every man craves recognition. Meaning derived from the lips of others. Purpose gleaned from praise. To turn your back on that is painful and leaves you vulnerable. Like standing on a temple top and knowing you could fly off and impress the world in an instant. Then turning, walking away, and praying for opportunities to wash the excrement off the feet of lesser mortals who would not think twice about flying off that temple top given half a chance.'
Up The Creek Having Burnt The Paddle by Pew Hadovood

- - - - - - - - - - -

The lead singer of the band The Giggheads is here! Mitch Levine! He's here! I can't believe it. Looks a little more restrained than when he's on MTV but it's definitely him. Whenever I see him I'm tempted to whistle a few lines from their version of *Born to run*, a recent global internet hit. Brother Ben from the kitchen tells me he's here to escape the madness of fame, which recently has upended him a little. Apparently his dad is a vicar and he's in no rush to embrace Christianity. But he likes being around the brothers here, and it's just a great place to hide from the press and autograph hunters. Now this is a tricky one 'cause I'm supposed to be here eschewing all that ordinary worldly stuff and I've found out he's here to do the same, but I'm desperate to somehow engineer a conversation with him. Perhaps we could chat about how we're escaping the attention of others. I don't actually have any Giggheads albums but I could become a fan, if I just got to know Mitch Levine a little better. Don't suppose his lead guitarist is here too by any chance? Phat Phingers Franklin?

I go down to the service in the chapel. I sit and stare at the weather-worn faces of the brothers. Saggy and creased from a million early mornings. The brothers have their services at all hours. They call them offices and give them glorious old Latin names like Matins, Lauds, Terce, Sext, None, Vespers and Compline. They know the prayers and hymns without looking and there's a sombre, singsong tone to their delivery. I try and lose myself in the sound but I can't stop thinking about Mitch. He's just a guy, probably tired and weary in the way that I am. Okay, rich and tired and weary. And known by anyone on the planet who looks at YouTube. But apart from that. We're the same. In which case he won't mind us chatting will he? Oh... why am I doing this? What can he give me that any other regular person can't? Apart from the usual 'I've met Mitch Levine in a monastery' anecdote to tell the others in the pub.

Why? Why do I want to tell the others in the pub? What's the point? Where's the gain? They'll probably make some joke and refuse to be impressed, and say they suppose I also met Phat Phingers too. If I did meet Phat Phingers that would really sort them out. Unbelievers. Brothers Ben, Basil and Aidan have stopped chanting. The chapel is deathly quiet. Somewhere there is the scratch of a mouse and somewhere else a stomach rumbles. Oh, it's mine. I need lunch. On the way out Brother Basil sneaks me over to one side.

'Don't forget that whisky,' he says with his cheeky grin.

We fix for the evening after tomorrow.

I decide to explore. I circle the main building and find a wooden hatch round the back, half open. It's tempting. Too tempting. I pull it back and slip inside. No idea what I'm looking for but I go down there anyway. I recall one of those 'choose your own adventure' books I read repeatedly as a boy. *The Secret of the Seven Stars.* Made me feel like I was a real detective on a real mystery. For a moment I get that feeling all over again. Along with the magic I felt when my dad once took me under the stage in our little local theatre. My father used to build sets for an amateur dramatic company. He worked under the stage in a mysterious basement, an Aladdin's cave of paint pots, plywood, brightly coloured scenery and hangers loaded with costumes. I recall to this day the feeling of adventure and curiosity as I descended those short wooden steps into that strange-smelling paradise. It comes right back now as I clamber down these steps. An old, white switch flicks on the lights, but they're ineffective, the glow is gloomy and yellow. I feel like Indiana

Jones down there. Indiana Jones in a musty, dusty basement, on the hunt for some lost monastic treasure. The Lost Habit of Death or something. I just need to find a discarded, charred torch, add some strips torn off the bottom of my shirt and set fire to it. Instead I just squint and wait for my eyes to adjust. A claustrophobic corridor looms before me. A line of doors leads off it. No doubt they'll be locked but I try the first handle anyway. It's open, the door swings back, I half expect Norman Bates's mother down there, a skeleton in a monk's habit, waiting, leering. But there's nothing, just a few old empty cardboard boxes. Bits of packing that once held fortified wine and sandals. I try the next room. There's a huge board on a couple of trestles with an old model Hornby train set laid out on it. A cluttered web of dusty black tracks and plastic figures. Trees, people, a level crossing. Suddenly I'm six again, lying under my bed listening to my train set rattle around above my head. It's laid out on my bed, on a board like this one, only a quarter of the size. This set is every kid's dream. Painted engines, sidings, stations, even a lake in the middle of it all. A spider emerges from the station master's office, squeezing its fat body through the window like an extra from a horror movie. It tramps across the lake, oblivious to the illusion of water there, climbs over a stray, brown guard's van, then knocks a pedestrian over before disappearing off the edge of the board. If I'd have filmed the bizarre occurrence I could have added the theme from Psycho and made a killing on YouTube. Which monk surrendered this when he arrived I wonder? And does anyone even remember that it's here? I can hardly slip it under my jumper and steal it away to my shed. It's bigger than my floor space there. I look for a power supply. There is one. I find a plug, push it on, flick the switch. Nothing. Something died a long time ago. Maybe the spider ate its way through a cable somewhere.

I leave the magnificent railway with a certain reluctance and try the next room. I leap back in shock, figures everywhere. Lifesize. Plaster statues. Saints staring at me. I shiver. These guys may have been heroes of the faith in their time but right now I feel like I'm in Madame Tussauds at midnight. And I want to be out of there. A footstep in the corridor. I turn. Another footstep and I catch sight of the frayed edge of a brown habit as it passes the door, a yellow sock protrudes from a standard issue sandal. I steel myself and stick my head out into the corridor. Nothing. Who was that? The owner of the train set? I've had enough adventures. I'll leave The Lost Habit of Death for someone else to find. I'm out of there.

Day 9: I Got Life

He stares at the ground. Kicks it with his foot. No life. Nothing. No sign that anything is growing here, nothing significant happening. Everywhere is barren. Yet he knows, he forces himself to know, other things are growing, other seeds are being sown and taking root. He is changing. His mind is alert, active, his spirit quicker, sharper than before. The wilderness may be lifeless right now but he is not. In the spring the rains come for a brief time, and then this place comes alive, if only for a short period. Well, his spring is right round the corner. And that will be short too. But life will appear all over the barren lands, all over the bad lands of Judea. All those who feel like this hard rocky ground will see life again. And those who want to keep a tight fist on the proceedings will find themselves swept over by the flood. They may not enjoy the drenching. It's uncomfortable standing around in wet clothes, watching others swim to freedom, but the rains will surely come. And choices will be made. He runs his hand over the ground. Hot, dusty, dry. But against all the odds there is still life there. He smiles to himself.

- - - - - - - - - -

My bed continues to fight back whenever I'm on it. In the wee small hours it creaks like a badly hung door. So after another restless night I decide to strike out for a long walk. The intensity of isolation comes and goes but I figure this will help. I pack a few things in my rucksack, slip down to the big house and beg a few slabs of bread and cheese from Brother Ben in the kitchen. He's easily the youngest monk here, and one who I suspect hides an iPod in the hood of his habit. Ben does most of the washing up here, lays the tables and cleans the floors in the kitchen and refectory. He also goes up ladders when things need fixing. He told me he wanted to be a stunt man when he was at school but then figured a monk's life more daring. He tells me he didn't have any sudden conversion, didn't suddenly see the light, he just sat down one day with Brother Basil and it made sense. He was a loner anyway and had grown up with a distant conviction that one day God would nab him for something. He's an Arctic Monkeys fan and is littered with tattoos. He has bits of the Bible etched all the way up both arms, apparently God's got his name tattooed on his hand so he thought he'd follow suit.

We chat about Mitch Levine for a bit while he cleans out a badly clogged drain. I notice his forearm sports the quote 'they shall be white as snow' as it disappears into a pile of grey and brown sludge. I pick his brains about where to walk, then leave him with his pile of muck. And then with Brother Ben's food and a few extra clothes I trek off to explore the far reaches of the moor. It's not long before I find myself standing before a modest statue of St Columba. I read the inscription on the base. It turns out this trail-blazing Irish monk was an author, scholar, monastery-founder, teacher and leader. He stands here now as a young man, tall and wiry, stick in his hand, and his robes flying behind him as he sets out on another adventure. He lived fifteen hundred years ago, but he doesn't look too bad on it. He looks young and confident. Two things I envy. Behind him there's a second statue. A guy going by the name of St Finian. Never heard of him. Couldn't have spread the faith like young Columba here. Couldn't have been the same kind of spiritual giant... I read the very short epitaph on the base. And suddenly I get it. *The man who trained St Columba.* Reminds me of an advert once where famous celebrities appeared on screen reciting names of people you'd never heard of. At the end of the advert the caption appeared – *No one forgets a good teacher.* I can recall two, a drama teacher who was cool and friendly, and a primary school teacher who took a keen interest in my writing skills. I'll never forget them.

Oddly, looking at these figures makes me think of Queen Victoria. I heard recently that there are statues of the great Empress of India all over the place, it's said that the sun never sets on her. And the reason? After unrest in the colonies she had loads of images of herself placed everywhere to remind people who was in charge. It wasn't an original idea. Back in the early days God said, 'I know, let's make people in our own image...' People like you and me, Columba and Finian. Images all over the place. Reminders of the God who hangs back in the shadows. Which I guess brings me back full circle to the good teachers we never forget. The people who have influenced us for the better. Those images of God who helped us and changed us and maybe didn't even know about it. I find myself hoping that there are some people out there who might include me on their list. Maybe a day when I smiled at them, or said the right thing, or listened to them, or shared a Mars Bar, or did something useful which helped them. I look to the blue sky and mutter a prayer about it.

'God please let me have made a difference. God please let me have been useful.'

I desperately want that. I don't want to be useless. Not right now. It matters more than ever that I have made my mark somewhere, left my thumbprint on this planet.

The sky of course is quiet in response. Good news and bad I suppose. No reassuring bright lights, but no thunderclap of destruction either. I watch a distant bird cavort and spin against the blue canvas. It looks to me like a falcon. For some unknown reason I find the sight of it hopeful and moving. I choke up. I don't know why. I don't understand. Something about the freedom and purpose of the creature perhaps. It continues to spin and dive and it takes quite a while to move out of sight. No idea how long I watch it. But I stand still for a long time.

Walking in the middle of nowhere I get the glorious revelation that no one has any idea where I am. I have no calls on my time, no pressures or responsibilities right now. And for a brief split-second I feel free. I shrug off the fears that chase like dogs around the wasteland of my head. I push them all away. I breathe in deeply. And I talk to myself. Something that's becoming a habit here, a whole lot of mumbling going on.

Seeds grow slowly, I say. It's a process that can't be hurried. Microwaves won't help, a greenhouse may make some difference to a tomato plant, but it won't hurry an oak tree along. If the best kind of people are like trees beside a stream, tapping into the reserves of life-giving water, then they'd better be in it for the long-haul. This is no fast-food ride. The best kind of development takes place a little each day, often in minute amounts, and in the dark as well as the light. In the sun, the rain, the snow, the driving wind. The growing goes on. And the many conditions bring on the multi-faceted development.

I stop talking and glance around. Still alone. No one there. But everywhere there is quiet determined life as things grow. Silently, without fuss or glamour. Life goes on developing. And one day someone else will walk this way, talk to themselves about life, and stand in the shade of a tree that right now is no more than a hidden seed in the ground. I like that.

I walk on. I talk again. My sermonising is going well. Not sure it will actually change anything in any way but it's keeping me entertained. My tale takes me back in time ten years, to a strange time in the twilight world of movies. I used to work in the world of cinema. And so I'd like to tell you incredible tales of making movies and rubbing shoulders with the stars. But I can't. I wasn't even a projectionist. When I say I worked in the world of cinema, I should say I worked in the foyer of one. Sweeping up popcorn, mopping the carpets, scraping up bubblegum and carrying bags of sick down to the basement bins. The most incredible tale I can tell you is that I once got trapped in the lift with one of those bags of vomit. Oh, and I once nearly stepped inside the same lift but spotted at the last minute that it had vanished into thin air. One more step and I'd have been spread thinly across the underground car park, like ketchup on concrete. But that's it, the full extent of my big screen adventures from those dark days. Most of the time I put on my multiplex uniform, served ice cream, weighed pick'n'mix, and felt depressed. I was also scared of the rest of the staff who were all half my age. You see I didn't want to be there. I wanted to be on the other side of the screen, working in Hollywood, writing blockbusters and cashing cheques. Disappointment didn't quite sum up the extent of my feelings about the wreckage of my ravaged dreams. Eighteen months in that job wasn't as tough as forty days in the desert, but it was a dead ringer of a wilderness for me. I had no idea at the time, but I was in training.

It changed me. Forever.

It's a cliché to say that which doesn't kill you makes you stronger, all I know is that this catastrophe affected me. Up until that point I thought Christianity was about success. In fact, I thought the two words were interchangeable. To be Christian was to be successful. At life. Family. Marriage. Career. Money. Behaviour. Well, I wasn't successful, I had never been successful. Carrying bags of sick was part of the process that helped me see that clearly. I was in a bad place, I wanted to run away, I wanted to deny my faith, yet I was still a Christian. If I were now to choose the Bible verse that sums up why I'm a follower of Jesus, I would look to a couple of verses in John's biography of Jesus. Jesus does a massive miracle, feeds a Wembley-sized crowd of people, and no revival breaks out. In fact the opposite occurs, everyone deserts him, everyone except a small troubled group of close mates. Jesus turns to them with a heavy heart and asks if they're going to run away too. To which good old Peter replies, 'Where could we go? You have the words of life.' Or in other words, 'We'd like to, but we can't think of anywhere else to go.'

Sometimes it seems like that. God's in my veins. I carry the Jesus who knew and understood failure everywhere I go. Nowhere else to go. Other words are good, other words are helpful, amusing, thought-provoking, kind, compassionate, mind-bending, profound, probing. But it's Jesus who has the words of life. That's how it seems to me, and loss and pain and failure have only reinforced that. A disintegrating marriage and a lost baby have only made it seem clearer than ever.

Certain seeds grew in my life while I was pulling bubblegum from cinema seats. They may not have grown in any other climate. But I didn't know anything was happening. The change went on while I carried on putting on my multiplex uniform and sweeping popcorn. Not only was it unseen, it actually didn't look like growth at all. It looked like desolation. To be cinematic for a moment, my daily existence looked to me like Maximus's home in the movie *Gladiator*. The faithful Roman officer returns to find his land scorched and his family dead. Like Job. And probably a little like Jesus on his worst day in the wilderness. But I couldn't see it at the time. I had no idea what was growing. I had no idea *anything* was growing. This wasn't my kind of plan at all.

Jesus may have been aware of the changes developing within him during his wilderness phase, but it may be that he only began to discover the extent of those changes later, as he took up his life again. As I stand here now, watching gulls dive and waves assault the shore, I realise that some changes cannot be rushed. They need time. All I can do is keep going, and keep deliberately setting my face in the direction of God's kingdom.

Hang on a minute. Where am I? Sea has suddenly crashed into the picture, way below me. The land has run out and I stand in silence looking down. Way down. Surf and rocks and the sound of the ocean crash about below. I'm on a cliff-edge. When did I reach the end of the earth here? How far have I walked? Is this just some bleary-eyed wilderness vision? Who knows, it doesn't matter. I'm in this place in this time. I could jump. It's a thought that often crosses my mind when I stand near a cliff edge. Not for any desperate suicidal reason, just because it's one of the things I could do. I mean… who would miss me now? Not the woman I once loved, and my family have all gone now. I have a cousin I haven't seen in years. Brother Basil wants another whisky with me I suppose. I do want to see him again. And I'm desperate for a chinwag with Mitch Levine, but he doesn't know that. So I stand on the edge of the land for a while and watch my boots push some fragile bits of cliff over the edge. Life can seem suddenly precarious sometimes. I can see myself falling, spinning in the air, turning upside down as I go. Am I still conscious, when exactly do you black out falling off a cliff like this… what happens?

I'm wet. It's raining. When did it start to rain? And that wind? When did that pick up? I shiver. I look down and see I'm standing in a puddle. My baseball boots are soaking. Like a couple of saturated sponges. I shake them off. A gust of wind hurls rain in my face. This is not good. What happened to the sunshine and the glory of God and my peaceful 'at one with the world' feelings? Without thinking I turn from the cliff edge and start tramping back. Which direction did I come in? Can't remember. Just walk. It'll warm you up and dry you out. Grief I'm wet, and getting wetter. When did this rain start? When? When? It's horrible. I pull an extra jumper from my bag and somehow wrestle it on as the wind shoves me around like a piece of old litter. I walk on. There's mud everywhere now. The moor is a mess. Am I going round in circles? Maybe. Can't figure it. What can I see? Nothing. 'Cause I'm out here in the middle of nowhere and no one knows where I am. Help! No one knows where I am! I don't want that! I don't want to be out here with no one else having any idea of my whereabouts. I need help. I need rescuing. What am I going to do? I'll die out here. I don't want to die! I want to be alive. I walk on, start to run, can't see much 'cause the rain is battering my eyes, forcing me to shut the lids more often than open them.

I have a vision of myself curled up on the moor all night, slipping in and out of consciousness, shivering and covered in goat dung. It's not a nice picture. It drives me on. Where am I? Where am I? Did Jesus get lost in his wilderness? Oh stop thinking spiritual thoughts! Just get on with getting back.

Day 10: Bad

'Jesus was going to reappear as a rabbi, a carpenter transformed without ever going to college or getting the right schooling. Educated in the University of Life, the School of Hard Knocks. To prepare him for a life of humility, compassion and forgiveness, his education required facing up to himself. And to the dark side of life. They say a priest's faith is taken apart at theological seminary in order to prepare him for what will hit him like a truck in life. If that is so, then the desert was Jesus's theological seminary. The wilderness was his ten ton truck.'
Up The Creek Having Burnt The Paddle by Pew Hadovood

- - - - - - - - - - -

I've moved my mattress onto the floor. I dragged it from the iron springs and slammed it onto the stained floorboards. At three o'clock this morning. I was so tired of the guttural screams from the bedsprings. At four I was woken by a draught coming from who knows where chilling my face. At five o'clock a fierce creature was scratching at the door. At six water was dripping from a secret crack in the ceiling onto my feet. This wasn't the peaceful retreat I'd had in mind. It's chaos in here, in my head and in the cabin. And now, as I lie here at seven staring at my Bible I find myself reading about another man on a mattress on the floor whose life is in chaos. Only this one can't get up. I read a while ago that in Jesus's day if you were sick or in trouble people thought that you'd brought it on yourself by doing something pretty bad. Hmm. So what did I do to earn this bed? No comment. Back to the story. Four mates bring this guy to Jesus to cure him and what's the first thing Jesus says? 'You're forgiven.' No blame culture here. No inquiry about what the guy's done. Jesus cuts through the people's bad theology and forgives the guy everything. Reminds me of another time when Jesus and his mates meet a blind guy and the first thing they ask Jesus is, 'Whose fault was it? Who did some really bad stuff? Him or his family?' Again the blame culture in action. And again Jesus sidesteps the whole issue and just heals him. On this occasion, with the man on the mobile bed, the religious leaders start kicking up a fuss about how you can't just forgive sins like that. So Jesus asks a great, gobsmacking question. 'Okay then, which is easier, to say you're forgiven? Or to say you're cured, get off your mat and start training for the Olympics?' Well er... actually Jesus, sometimes it seems easier to try saying 'you're cured' than to appear a naïve pushover and just go round forgiving people. Jesus is way too liberal about these things. Can't go round randomly dishing out kindness in a blame culture, you'll get crucified.

Thinking of kindness reminds me of Brother Basil. I think I should talk to him some more. I get off my mat and go for a walk. It's light outside but God's still turning the fader up. There's the smell of morning out there, and sunlight too, sneaking a look through the bushes and undergrowth. The last hangers-on from the dawn chorus are still chirping away. Suddenly I feel a lot less tired. I realise as I trudge through the damp ground that I haven't read a blog or watched a YouTube clip in over a week. I don't know what's happening in the world of Facebook, Twitter or LinkedIn. I am totally LinkedOut. Totally. All I have are these birds and the sunlight and a few real people to talk to. I walk on, kicking at the knotty clumps of grass and the stray stones. The sun gets higher. The warmth encourages my soul, chases away some of the chill. No doubt about it. The sunlight is definitely starting to look like God's glory to me. The sun shines on the great and the good and the bad and the ugly. That's what Jesus said, or words to that effect. It's indiscriminate, and I'm starting to believe the glory of God is everywhere. In some places it's easier to spot. Like here and now in the quiet and the beauty and the space of a morning on the moor. But perhaps I'm just more aware of it because I don't have Facebook and Twitter to distract me. A radio doesn't stop existing just because I'm more interested in the TV. The glory of God keeps breaking through and it's up to me to spot it. To take a brief millisecond to find the light and stand in it. That said I look down now and I'm in a cow pat. Fortunately it's an old crusty thing, and my baseball boots are barely scathed, but still, it's unfair to be bathing in the glory of God and then find yourself smeared with dung.

As I wipe my boots on the dewy grass I think about Ezekiel, my favourite prophet. The guy who took a cow pat like that and set fire to it so he could fry up his full Israelite breakfast. Presumably no bacon, sausages or black pudding in that. Maybe some fried pomegranates, sautéed figs and some Cumberland pottage.

Evening. Time for that whisky. I'm off to see Brother Basil and his tumbledown cottage. It's dark and I fear there may be man traps buried amongst the debris in his garden so I tread carefully. I also fear an ambush from his chickens. All is well, I get to his door without losing a leg. He's waiting, the door pulls back before I can knock. I follow the little man into his wreck of a study and fall deep into one of his chairs. There's a bottle on the little table.

I ask Brother Basil about St Columba, he says I should ask Brother Aidan, he has a brain the size of a planet when it comes to the old saints. Knows about Finian too, and his namesake Aidan. I'm not so sure, he looks fierce. I tell Brother B who laughs. 'He is fierce,' he says, 'but he's good too.' And he winks at me in a C S Lewis kind of way. 'Let's christen this whisky,' he says and he winks in a Johnny Walker kind of way.

The drink loosens me up and it doesn't take long to move from the weather and the waffle to the grittier stuff. Small talk has always been a blind spot for me, in fact it's this that brings us to another key place.

'I feel I have this disconnection inside. Some wiring that doesn't quite connect up.'

He waves a hand to urge me on. I take another sip. The liquid bites.

'Well, it's like I can't quite work out what other people want from me, I get into a conversation with someone and I end up spending much of my time just trying to work out what they're saying. And what I'm supposed to say back to them. And by the time I've worked it out it's become a mathematical equation, a case of just getting it right, and the conversation is dead in the water. And to muddy those waters further, there's a part of me that at the same time, doesn't care anyway. I have no interest in talking about the inconsequential things, the things that to my mind will be just the same tomorrow and the day after. I can't muster the energy to be interested. And yet... and yet...' I lean forward in my chair, 'I care about people. I'm convinced caring for other people is a major part of Christianity. Not just getting saved, or converting the bloke down the chippie, but really caring about people. After all, how can I convert anyone if I don't care about them. You see I've seen too many people out there wanting to Christianise everyone...' I'm really warming to my subject now, 'but they don't seem to really see others as genuine, unique individuals. Precious to God. And what did Jesus say? Love each other. What did Paul say? The greatest thing is love. Oh, I don't know. What am I getting worked up about? That's off the subject anyway.'

Brother Basil raises both eyebrows. 'Is it? Isn't it another part of your struggle to connect? When you see others not bothering to do that? Not having compassion.'

I shrug. Maybe.

'I just don't feel a part of anything. I feel cut adrift. Out to sea. And the older I get the worse it gets. You know that old adage, 'No man is an island'? Well, I think I'm slowly breaking free of the mainland and becoming just that.'

'You've been through upheaval. Don't forget that. Marriage. Baby. Job. You're still, as they say nowadays, processing it all. You must give yourself time.'

'That's what I'm here for, to get fixed!'

'Ah well, being fixed and giving yourself time are not the same thing. Being fixed sounds awfully like just dispensing with another problem. But you're not a problem, you're a carefully-crafted muddle, you're a uniquely defined ragbag of a person. Don't be offended, it's best to be clear on that. Know the truth and let it set you free. Allow yourself to fail at this thing called life for a while. Allow yourself to drift off the mainland.'

'But I can't, I'm a Christian!'

Brother Basil laughs. He actually laughs, and it's a belly laugh too. Not just a polite chuckle. A genuine guffaw.

'And the best Christians know they are failures,' he says with a smile the size of Sydney Harbour. 'I'm a terrible failure. St Paul was a terrible failure. Read Romans 7. It's all about his lack of success. And he's not just pretending, or if he is then he's telling huge great fibs, and that makes him a failure! You remember I mentioned about those folks in church with their stridently happy choruses? Well I think that's what concerns me, I wonder if they sing so loudly and intensely to somehow drown out the reality of their own failings. To put on hold all those embarrassing, tripping-up-over-your-own-feet moments. You know, those times when you're getting ready for bed and the phone goes and you try and reach it with your trousers around your ankles and the next thing you know you're sprawled half-naked in the dining room hoping the curtains aren't open. Those moments set us free, they connect us with reality, and with the God of reality. Don't be frightened of them. Let them happen and then remind yourself that God is with you as much then, when you're sprawled on the carpet with your trousers round your ankles, as he is when you're kneeling in church with a benign smile on your face. It's the only way. More whisky?'

I go back to my shed and read Romans 7. It's true. Brother B is not wrong. It's littered with the longings of a man on the edge. A man seeing himself clearly and wrestling with the image. Most people quote the answer to his question 'Thank God! The answer is in Jesus Christ our Lord.' But the question is a lot longer, takes up a lot more space and there's hope in the very asking. It's the profound truth. The one we are all left with. Brother B is right. Paul's in trouble here, the same kind of trouble I'm in, we're all in. We've signed up to a life of contradiction and it's uncomfortable. We believe in peace but we're not peaceful. We believe in truth but we're dishonest. We believe in justice but we're not very just. The armour of God looks great on the hanger but it's an ill-fitting outfit. We have to keep hitching it up and adjusting that old belt of truth. The straps of the breastplate keep slipping and the helmet's a little too big.

Day 11: Sowing The Seeds Of Love

He has seen farmers over the years throwing seeds. Chased round the fields and pathways as a boy, trying to find some of them. Thorns often got in the way and the birds too. Hosea. Why's he suddenly think about Hosea? His thoughts are getting uncontrollable. Jumping all over the place. Hosea. Hosea. Hosea... Hosea talked about seeds, he remembers that story now. That old heartbroken prophet who lost his wife twice, first to adultery and then to death. He came through his own wilderness and saw the future clearly. 'Plant the good seeds of righteousness,' he shouted from the street corners, 'and you will harvest a crop of love. Plough up the hard ground of your hearts, break up that arid, solid surface, for now is the time to seek the Lord, track him down so that he may come and shower righteousness on you.' Could Hosea see a nearby sun-baked farmer showering the ground with seeds as he said it? Maybe. Good seeds. The farmer throws them out, then it's up to the ground. Like Hosea's words out looking for good ears. This ground here is resistant, but there are patches of other soil out there. Fertile land. Some of it besieged by thorns, some of it beaten into a path by the feet of pilgrims looking for something better. Birds hang around waiting to peck up anything that comes their way, eating the seeds instead of the fruit. Always a danger. The seed lands and before it can produce anything it's gone. Pecked and swallowed and the bird doesn't think twice. Though it may have taken away the chance of new life altogether. He stares out over the barren landscape. His mouth is dry. He needs to find water. His thoughts are racing, his mind swimming. Needs to focus. He shuts his eyes and pictures all those farmers he watched as a boy. All that seed sown. All that possibility.

The farmer sows and doesn't know about the process that follows. He sows and waits and works and gets on with his life. And other things happen, circumstances twist and turn. And one day he glances over at his field and sees a crop has started to appear. And sometimes a single seed produces a massive tree. All the other seeds may come to nothing, but a single seed can produce the kind of fruit that millions feed on. Then those birds don't scratch around on the paths for wasted seed, they come and nest and build homes for their families. Futures for their young. He is rambling, he knows it. Tiredness is taking its toll. Being alone so long, being hungry for a while. So hungry. So alone. Who's that figure in the distance? Why is someone coming all the way out here to meet him?

- - - - - - - - - -

My cabin is eleven feet by twelve. I know it well, I've paced it out. It contains my complaining bed, the mattress on the floor, a square trestle table, a lamp, a kettle, a sink, a wardrobe and that armchair. And I know now why the backs of the arms are so scarred. It's from other inmates clawing at the wood in their efforts to stay sane. I know the details of this room well. The gaps between the floorboards, the five stains on the ceiling, the fourteen separate cracks in the walls. The splintery beams crisscrossing overhead. Eleven days has been a long time. I spend more time outside than in right now, even though the weather has turned foul. The monastery has a square, stone quad with benches, plus a library, a chapel and a dining hall. These all provide escape from my cell, though I've yet to track down the library. I think it's like Harry Potter's platform 9 ¾. You have to run at the right wall and risk knocking your teeth out. I have visited my outside toilet though. I haven't used an outside loo since I was six when my grandfather still had one at his terraced house. But now even this is a welcome break from the four walls. Indiana Jones once got encased in a tomb where the walls were closing in on him. I know how he feels. Right now I have plenty of moments when I could give up and go home. My previous workmates would think I'm mad if they knew I was here. Who willingly goes to a place like this? What is there to be gained? There are so many useful things I could be doing. Time out with God? Surely someone's having a laugh.

I think I'm going a bit crazy. I get ideas in my head, mad ideas, and then spend an hour trying to get rid of them but of course I can't because it's like telling yourself not to think of an exploding arm. That's all you can then think about. What happens if your arm suddenly exploded? If somehow the atoms started to attack each other and the whole limb split and burst like an over ripe marrow with a stick of dynamite in it. Like I say it's madness but I seem stuck with that and a million other preposterous ideas that won't go away. And I can't decide which is worse – the thought rattling around my head again and again, or the fear of the thought. Needless to say it infects everything, I try and read or go for a walk and it's there in the background like a badly tuned radio, static in my head. I've had it before, usually the kind of thing that rears its head when I have too much time on my hands. And what do I have right now? Exactly. Twenty-nine more days of this and they'll be burying me in Brother Basil's junk garden. I can't help wondering if Jesus was haunted by restless images from his carpentry days. Did he find himself repeatedly thinking of those moments when he'd hammered his thumb by mistake, did he replay again and again and again the conversations he'd had in the temple when he'd bantered with the scribes and rabbis?

What did Jesus do with his loneliness out there in the wilderness, rehearse the sermon on the mount? Tell himself stories to keep his brain active? Practise turning water to wine? I grab my e-reader and flip to *The Dangerous Book of Heroes*. Astonishing tales of strength and courage and character. The undercover women of the *Special Operations Executive* captured in world war two and held in solitary confinement went to all kinds of creative lengths to stay sane. One woman, Odette Braily, designed clothes for her family and redecorated the homes of her friends, all in her imagination. She rotated her skirt one inch each day so that the wear on it would be even. All under the loneliness and stress of hostile imprisonment.

Sleeping isn't going great either. Last night I kept dreaming that God was here in the shed with me, like a large, black woman with flour on her hands. He kept asking me my favourite food and then serving it up, so we could sit down and chat over it. I dreamt it three times, and each time I woke up with a jolt and the smell of roast beef in my nostrils, expecting him to be right here. I was starting to feel pretty full by the time daylight came round. I think the isolation may be getting to me.

The recurring dream makes me wonder whether I shouldn't expect more. I'm in a holy strip of England. A *thin place*. A piece of earth where the divide between heaven and earth is narrow. Surely I should be getting some kind of close encounter. I may be going stir crazy but I spend a good hour lying on my bed, staring at the ceiling, willing the face of God to appear in the cobwebs and cracks. And then the thought spooks me, what if he did appear? Wouldn't that mean instant death, thunderbolts on God's part and heart attacks on mine?

The Bible speaks constantly of God's presence, or rather, the bumbling writers who concocted the famous good book speak constantly of God's presence. Prime Ministers and peasants, heroes and villains come across him in the most unexpected of places. Yet he remains mostly invisible. Occasionally misfits like Moses and Ezekiel get gob-smacking visions and glimpses and bump into angels thinly disguised. But much of the time the presence of God plays out in the ordinary glory of friendship, coincidence and the frenzy of daily living. I'm lying here demanding God show up and perform like a talented pet. Yet far greater people than me have been satisfied with the presence of God secreted in normalcy, in the regular life that God himself created and maintains. I have the faith to find God in the supernatural, but have I got it to find him in the mundane?

Jesus himself seems to find God in farmers sowing seeds and widows putting a penny in the collection. Hardly big screen revelations. A lot more Mike Leigh than Steven Spielberg. Little secrets about the kingdom. A man hurls seeds everywhere, God's healthy ideas, and some of them find their target. This telling tale must surely be in the top five in *the most famous parables of all time* chart, along with the prodigal son, the two builders and the good Samaritan. It's one of only two parables Jesus explained. He had a lot to say but did most of it using stories that required concentration and a curious mind. Pearls wrapped up in gripping yarns, so the pigs couldn't trample them. Were there more stories that never made it into the good book? Did Jesus spend a lot of his desert time writing best sellers in the dust? You know – the parable of the school for wizards, the parable of the teen-vampires and the parable of the girl with the dragon tattoo.

Personally I like the one about the worldwide web. You can't actually see it, but you know it's there because of all those web pages. God is like the internet. All around but you can't actually see him or touch him, what you can see is what he provides. The people, creatures and places. God's web pages. You and me. He's also like a SatNav, forever patient when you take the wrong turn, ready to say a million times, with the same gentle tone, 'Turn around when possible.' That is unless you have Basil Fawlty as the voice on your Sat Nav in which case the parable falls apart a bit.

Somewhere in the Judean wilderness, one day in the future, two ten year-olds will be playing football when they discover the scrolls that contain these long lost gems. I'm sure of it.

Day 12: Next To Me

'We don't do well with the invisible God. We want solidity, which is probably why the old master crafter gave us crosses and crucifixes, cups of wine and chunks of bread. We need our symbols. The best symbol is probably that found in the ancient desert crossing, the pillars of cloud and fire, two uncontainable representatives of God. We see them but we cannot box them, pin them down or measure them. The best image we have of course is you, and the person next to you. We are the best piece of multimedia the creator has, and when we show courage, kindness, patience and humility, we do a good impression of God.'
Up The Creek Having Burnt The Paddle by Pew Hadovood

- - - - - - - - - - -

Bumped into Brother Ben on my way up to the chapel this morning. Was feeling particularly down when he came bounding up looking a strange mixture of excited and embarrassed.

'I er...' he paused. 'I was thinking yesterday,' he started, 'and I had this idea, I don't know if I did the right thing, but...'
He held out his hand, there was an mp3 player in it and a couple of tiny silver earphones.

'It's just an old player but I don't use it anymore and actually, it's what's on it really. After our chat about music the other day, you know, and Mitch Levine and The Giggheads and everything. Well it's got their stuff on it. I just couldn't get it out of my head. I hope you don't mind and I know you're getting away from everything so you could wait and listen to it when you get home if you like. It's just a little... gift... really.'
He gave a final flinch and a grin. I took the player and turned it in my hands.

'A gift?' I said.
He nodded.

'Hope that's okay?' he said.
'It's more than okay,' I replied. 'In fact it's perfect.'
'Really? But it's just an old one. It works and everything.'

'Great! No it really is perfect. You see…'

'Yes?'

'Today's my birthday. And I thought I wouldn't get anything. From anyone.'

He stared and his mouth dropped open.

'I mean it was fine,' I hurried on. 'I wasn't going to tell anyone. In a way it was an experiment. I wanted to see what it was like to have a birthday that… wasn't. If you see what I mean. So this is extraordinary.'

'Amazing! I just got this hunch to do something. Happy Birthday! Ooh, late again for chapel. Come on.'

And we ran, me and this gift bearing monk and my new old mp3 player.

I'm sitting here in chapel now not taking much of it in. Just turning the little mp3 player over and over in my fingers. It's scratched and scarred and just about one of the best presents I ever had. I did want to try having a birthday with no celebration or recognition. But I didn't really. Not when I woke up this morning and I was cold again in my shed. How many people always wake up cold and alone on their birthdays? Maybe millions.

Did they celebrate birthdays in Jesus's day? When was his birthday again? Ah yes… that would be 25th December of course… except it wouldn't be. That was just a date nicked from the Romans. A useful one – the Feast of the Unconquerable Sun. The celebration of the promise of light and warmth returning to the earth after long winters. Appropriate then that Jesus should be the unconquerable son. And he got presents too. Famous ones. Gold, frankincense and myrrh. Maybe a lamb too if all those pictures of the shepherds are to be believed. What did his mum and dad do with that gold? Could have been worth a fortune to them. Maybe they put it into Jesus's college fund? Or bought a house perhaps when they came back from Egypt and went to live in Nazareth?

Later. I go out walking with The Giggheads. It's the kind of album that you know you're going to love even though you recognise nothing on it. They're all celebratory, guitar-jangling tunes with bits of harmonica and sax thrown in for good measure, and lyrics that celebrate life and the strange things about it. The Giggheads are good! I'm a fan. I want to meet the lead singer. I want to chat to Mitch Levine. Is he still here? Is he?

I go wandering down to the chapel quad 'for some time out' on the off chance that I might meet Mitch. But I don't. I do see Ben again though and he grins and asks me if I like the album.

'Perfect,' I say, 'It's perfect. Real feelgood stuff.'

He nods, with his head and shoulders, a real happy big agreement.

'I thought you'd get it,' he says.

He's tipping dirty water from a huge metal bucket, a real waterfall of grey liquid and soggy off-white food scraps.

'Been cleaning the floor, gets disgusting,' he says, 'toilets are next.'

He grins again. 'And they say a monk's life ain't glamorous.' He gives me a thumbs up and leaves me, wandering back with the bucket swinging from his left fist. I feel suddenly stupid and small. I came looking for a celebrity and found a hero instead. Who needs Mitch Levine when you can talk to Brother Ben. I shove in the earphones and wander the long way back to my shack so I can hear all of *Stairway to Devon*, six minutes of sheer unbridled rock 'n' roll happiness. I play it loud, and find myself singing along, not caring who hears.

It's Mitch Levine. And he's standing right in front of me. And he's grinning at me. Where did he come from? Where? Where? How can he be suddenly here making me feel like an idiot just because I like one of his songs. I hastily pull the plugs from my ears. The song plays on in the background.

'*Stairway*,' he says pointing at the dangling earplugs. He's chewing gum.

I nod. 'Sorry about the noise.'

'You calling my music noise?' He laughs but doesn't say anything else.

'What er... when.... I mean why... er... are you....are you having a good time here?' It's all I can think of, as much as I refuse to be cowed by a celebrity, actually meeting one turns me into a gibbering wreck.

'Not really,' he says and he kicks the ground. 'Kind of regretting it. Came to get away from it all, but I realise now I hate being away from it all. Can't live with it, can't live without it.'

I nod as if I know what he means.

'So quiet. So, so quiet.' He looks around, pushing the gum around his mouth with his tongue. 'Too quiet.' He gestures with his hands and spins a full 360 degrees on his heels. 'I came to find myself but I can't catch sight of me at all. I think I left last week. I mean, why would I stay? Nothing's happening. Nothing.'

'Maybe you should talk to one of the brothers,' I say.

He grimaces. 'Supposed to, Brother Boffin or something or other.'

'Basil?'

'Yea, that's him. Any good?'

'Yes, he's good. Better than good. He might even offer you a whisky.'

Mitch's eyebrows go up a floor. He's wearing a purple jacket, designer jeans, and winkle pickers. Together it probably cost more than my car, but he looks a wreck.

'You write such happy songs,' I say.

He grimaces again. 'Yea. I try. Maybe that's why I'm so miserable, I put all the good stuff on the page. Left with nothing for myself.'

'My wife used to say that the fruit you bear is picked by other people, which is why comedians can be so bloody miserable.'

He laughs. 'She *used* to say it?' he asks.

'Well probably still does, but she's not my wife anymore.'

'Oh, I know that feeling. I know it three times over.'

He turns and starts to walk away, then looks back. 'Is that *Long John Silver's Missing Leg* you're listening to? Check out track five. You'll like it. It's my favourite right now.'

He saunters off looking somehow too small and creased to be a rock star. I got my chat with the famous Mitch but I felt more alive meeting Ben as he threw out the dirty water. Hope he chats to Brother Basil. I wander back wondering why I felt the need to swear just 'cause I was talking to Mitch Levine.

Day 13: Still Waters

'Was he angry? In the wilderness, faced with all the kingdoms of the world and the offer of having them, did he get mad?

He got mad on at least two other occasions. When he went back to the temple, the system he'd grown up with, and saw yet again how it was uncaring, hard-hearted, money-making. Everything God was not. He got mad that day. Mad enough to karate tables and drop-kick the money changers' unbalanced scales. He is famous for the whip and the scene he made that day. And what about the other time, the time he stared death in the face. When he saw two sisters who were in grave danger of losing their home, their livelihood, their inheritance because they were unmarried and an age-old law meant a dead brother couldn't decide for himself where to pass on his wealth. He got infuriated that day. Deeply, gut-wrenchingly mad. And he showed it, the experience drove him to lose his cool in another way, not turning tables now, instead vomiting angry tears, groaning and spitting with righteous rage at the way life could be.

So was he enraged at the deceptive lies in the wilderness, this saviour who could feel things very deeply indeed?'

Up The Creek Having Burnt The Paddle by Pew Hadovood

- - - - - - - - - - -

I walk in the dark listening to track five of *Long John Silver's Missing Leg* – Mitch Levine's favourite track. *Angry As A Slug In Salt.* It sounds like a sad, slow-death of a track, but it's not, it's anything but, it's a glorious celebration of a man laughing at his own absurd tendency to get apoplectically enraged at the smallest crumbs of life. Inserts that fall from the *Radio Times* get a mention, as do people who slurp their coffee in public, mobile phones in the cinema, breaking wind in confined, crowded spaces and pompous, self-righteous adverts for men's designer perfume.

'What else makes you angry?'

I'm sitting in Brother Basil's overcrowded study again, whisky in hand.

'What do you mean?'

'Well, what we were talking about the other day, you were clearly annoyed about some of that.'

'Me.'

'Yes you.'

'No. I mean *me*. I make me angry. Because I can't be what I think I should be. When I was a raving evangelical Christian I used to talk about converting everyone but I didn't do it. Now I talk about compassion, but I'm not compassionate. I talk about helping others, but I don't do it. Sometimes I hate myself for it.'

Silence. I wait for the wise words, but there are none.

'Do you ever hate yourself?' I ask, mostly to break the silence.

'I'm often disappointed. Frequently so. But I do try and remind myself that God isn't. It's not easy. What else makes you angry?'

'When I was a young boy, about twelve, I used to buy a packet of Crawfords Cheddars biscuits, take them home and sit in front of the radio listening to music and recording my favourite tracks. It was bliss. Paradise.' I say.

Brother Basil nods. He gestures with his hand for more.

'That's it,' I say, 'I just loved it. Nothing more than that. I think I'm probably a closet reclusive at heart.' There seems to be a certain irony about that. A reclusive in a closet.

'Hence forty days living in a shed,' says Brother B.

I shrug. Nod. Smile. Shrug again.

'And... you wish you could still do that?'

I wince and nod. 'I have a packet of Cheddars in my shed.'

He nods.

'So you're angry that life won't let you do that anymore. It won't let you hide in your cave with your radio and your biscuits.'

'I'm annoyed that my faith won't let me do that.'

'So am I,' he says, 'though with me it was Custard Creams and *Jennings*. Remember Jennings? *Jennings Goes to School*? Darbishire, Temple, Venables? Linbury Court prep school? No? Shame. It meant a lot to me because I went to schools like that. A world that's long gone now. Ho hum. Do you ever wish you could turn back time?'

'Of course. All the time. I'd be prepared for what's coming and not look such an idiot.'

'Life would lack its surprises though,' says Brother Basil.

Exactly.

'I wish I could restore my system to the factory settings,' I say and Brother B sits back, eyebrows high.

'You know, like you can with a computer. You can reset the thing. Actually, it's better than that. You don't have to go all the way back, you can just reset it to a certain point just before it all went wrong. Life needs that kind of programme.'

'Do you think the point of life is to get it right then?' asks Brother Basil.

'If you don't want to hurt too many people or get damaged yourself, yes. I'd like to be able to go back and set it heading in the right direction, so it ends up the way I expected it to be when I was a kid. I just want a little more control of it, that's all. To look less like Johnny English and more like James Bond.' A silence. I break it. 'Did you always expect to be a monk?'

'Not at all, and neither did my wife. You see - I was married.'

I wince. 'There you go, that's what I mean. Now I want the ability to reset that conversation and try it again.'

Brother Basil laughs.

'D'you fancy a swim?' he asks suddenly and he leaps up.

I stare.

'Come on.'

'I don't have a costume.'

'We'll go in these.'

He dives into a cupboard wedged somehow between the stacks of books and hurls a pair of long-johns at me.

'But it's freezing.' Plus we're going to look ridiculous. I don't say that last bit though.

He pours a couple more shots of brown liquid and hands me the glass. He clinks his against mine and knocks it back.

'You'll be fine!' he says. 'It's all that talk of *Jennings* – just the kind of thing he would do. Come on.'

I have no idea where I'm going. And it is very cold out there. This is not what I came to a monastery to do. We walk in the dark, Basil chatting away. I get visions of him suddenly disappearing down a black, boggy hole.

'There!'

He points. Water glistens up ahead.

'Not deep, just a little lake.'

'Not clean either.'

He waves his long-johns at me and we hop around pulling them on in the dark. I am so glad everyone I know in the world is not there to see this. Johnny English comes to mind again. I make doubly sure that I know where my discarded clothes are before turning my back on them. While I'm still checking there's a splash and I turn to see Brother Basil's head floating in the water.

'Ah! It's bracing! Ooh yes!'

There's nothing else for it. There could be eels in there, leeches, crocodiles, piranhas. But if I'm not to let an ageing monk get the better of me then I'd better get in and get cold. I walk on mud. My legs start to complain. I trudge further. Basil is splashing about.

'Just a few minutes!' he calls.

I'm at that point where a sane person goes no further. The water is over my knees. The only way in now is to fall forward. I won't do it. I don't have to. Why should I? I'm a sensible adult.

I fall in. The shock hits my body and I flail about to get warm. No chance. I swim like a three-year-old for a minute then brother Basil shoots up.

'Come on!' he yells and he leads me back out.

Back in his cottage as we dry ourselves off and fight our way back into clammy clothes he says,

'Now, if you knew that was coming, it wouldn't have been a surprise would it?'

Day 14: We Could Be Heroes

There is a strange figure standing in the early morning light. A shadowy image waiting by a rock. Who is this cautious person, hovering like moonlight on a vacant, shallow puddle? He moves a little closer, the figure moves too. He cannot make out the features. There is no smile, no expression at all. The man is lean, about five foot three or four, the map of his face not clear enough to tell if he is good-looking, grim, worn down, young or old. He steps a little closer again. Speaks at the stranger. There is no reply. Eventually he realises. He is looking at himself. A silhouette on a rock, yet more than a mere shape. A projection of the man he is becoming. Wiry, determined, intent. Yet smaller and less impressive than he remembers. He sighs and the image sighs. He does not look particularly attractive out there. He does not look much of a hero or a villain. He will blend in no problem. A man of his time and background. A country boy who should know his place. He looks at himself for a long time. He sits and the image sits. It barely seems possible that this thin figure of a man could change much of anything. A lizard slips across the face, the tail flicking as it goes. Somewhere a snake hisses. And isn't that a lion roaring in the background? A wild animal waiting to devour this insignificant Messiah?

- - - - - - - - - -

I finally pluck up the courage to go and see Brother Aidan. The Mick Jagger of these parts. As I walk along the meandering path and through the quad that leads to the big house I have images of his leathery face before me with his steel-sharp eyes and thin grey lips. He lives in a couple of rooms in the big house just above the refectory. I stand outside his huge study door, flex my knuckles for a while, then knock once. There is no answer, I wait for the longest time then raise my fist to knock again and it's as if he was waiting for that.

'Come,' he says, so I go in, my hand still hovering to knock that second time.

I feel as if I'm back at school and about to go and see the headmaster for some stupid stunt I pulled. Well, there are plenty to choose from. I turn the handle and walk into the dragon's den. What am I doing here? Brother Jagger is sitting at a huge desk, it looks as if a library has exploded across it. He clearly doesn't have an e-reader. For one insane moment I wonder about offering him mine. I say nothing.

Brother Jagger lifts his eyes, not his face, just his eyes.
    'Yes?' he says, and there are echoes of Severus Snape about him.
I glance around, trying my best to get my bearings. Brother Jagger/Snape/Aidan's study is immaculate. He may have all the books in the known world but he looks after them. Every inch of wall is lined with shelves and every inch of shelf holds a tidily ordered book. There are little labels every so often. *History. Biography. Spirituality. Science. Art. Harry Potter.* Harry Potter? Yes, it's true, Brother Snape has his own adventures up there. The hardbook adult versions, of course. They may even be Monk versions by the look of the dustjackets.
    'Yes?' he says again, this time lifting his face from his work.
I open my mouth, fortunately some words make it out. 'Brother Basil said er… well… you see, I'm seeing him while I'm here… you know to get my head straight… and… I asked him about Brother Columba. I mean Sister Columba. Sorry St Columba.' I stop, it's probably best to stop there. My hole is deep enough already.
Aidan's thin lips look as if they might just break a smile. They don't.
    'Columba?' he says, thankfully ignoring the rest of my monologue. A long pause, my life passes, I sense my beard growing, then, 'I'd love to talk about St Columba.'

And then he does smile, and suddenly his face is transformed, the leather softens and someone turns a light on behind the steel-grey eyes. Perhaps he won't kill me just yet. He rubs his hands together suddenly, I'm not sure if he's happy or just warming them, because I realise how cold his study is when he does it. He gestures towards a dodgy-looking chair on the other side of his desk.
    'Talk to me,' he says with the same kind of glee I have seen in Brother Basil.

I sit, the chair creaks for all its worth. Aidan laughs.

'Don't worry, a huge man sat in it last week and it survived.'

Maybe that's why it's on its last legs this week.

'Did you know his Norse name meant Black Bear?'

Who, the big man on the chair?

'Brother Columba. His name in old Norse was Kolban. Black Bear. I like that.' He leans forward in his seat, his eyes still alight. 'Black Bear! Now then, what's your question?'

'Well it's not so much a question, I saw the statues here in the grounds, and I know very little about the saints of old...'

Aidan claps his hands together and rubs them hard. His nails are bitten and chipped and his thumbs black near the quick as if he's hit them with a hammer.

'Now then, where to begin,' he says. He stands up and begins to walk around me. I shift to watch him circle, the chair creaks again. I cling onto it.

'Columba was born on December 7th 521, he...' Aidan stops and stares at me. 'You don't have a notebook,' he says.

I shake my head.

'But you should always have a notebook when talking of Columba and Aidan and the gang.'

He turns and reaches a wiry arm towards the shelf. With the kind of flurry reserved for conjurors he produces a fantastically battered brown book. He holds it up, it looks like it has been through a war zone. All scuffs and dents and frayed edges. He opens it, flips through it quickly then hands it to me.

'My father took this to the Spanish Civil War. The book came back, he sadly did not.' He shakes his head. 'No idea what he planned to write in it, he was killed before he could.'

My mouth falls open.

'But I can't take that...'

'Why not? Not good enough?'

No, the opposite of course.

He smiles again. 'Exactly,' he says, 'I want you to take the old saints seriously, many of them put their lives on the line so you can sit here today in that flimsy chair. Perhaps this battle-worn old book will remind you of their legacy.'

He hands me a pen and continues walking.

'Now, Columba...' and he spills out details as if they are kids coming out of school at the end of a summer's day. 'Born in Ireland in 521... the great-great-grandson of King Niall of the Nine Hostages... came over in 563 with twelve others... founded the monastery on Iona... seen as the reinvigorator of Celtic faith... trained at St Finian's and then under the bard Gemman... he was a poet and...'

Aidan seems to grow in stature as he talks, almost doing an impersonation of Columba as he paces. I do my best to keep up but it's no mean achievement.

And then his smile fades and suddenly the old Aidan is back, leathery face, steel eyes, thin lips. It's all back. And he drums his fingers gently and precisely as he waits for me to leave. Lesson number one, get him on the old saints and you've got a friend. Small talk? Forget it.

I walk back to my cabin deep in thought.

Day 15: Changes

'Change is never easy. And this period in the desert is all about that. It's a fermenting, a maturing, a brewing of strong ideas that will burst across the Judean countryside like spilt beer from a smashed barrel. The friendship of God will be felt in the land once again. The poor and the orphans will find help, and the hopeless will be blessed. Justice will be the flag, compassion the currency, and strangers and aliens will at last find a place to call home as the jaws of their godless oppressors lie shattered in the dust.'
Up The Creek Having Burnt The Paddle by Pew Hadovood

- - - - - - - - - - -

Mitch Levine has gone. Brother Ben tells me after chapel this morning. So my big chance has gone. My lurch for fame was brief and impotent. One chat after being caught out wailing to one of his songs. I think about the sad, lonely, trendy guy, who couldn't see the beauty in this place. I wonder whether he ever got to have a serious chat with Brother Basil, but I don't ask. Brother Ben asks me how it's going. We chat about the forgettable things very briefly, then he asks me if I think it'll change me being here. I'm not sure what to say so he starts talking about pop music. His eyes light up and he says he has never forgotten an old episode of *Top of the Pops* from 1977. He says he caught it on the internet a while back. On iPlayer. He claims it opened his eyes to something about God.

'*Top of the Pops* opened your eyes to something about God?' I repeat.

'Yea, kind of, about how people don't like change. Back in '77 there was revolution in the air.'
I know. I was there. It was the Queen's Silver Jubilee year and to celebrate a certain band brought out their version of *God Save The Queen*.

'Yea well, watching the clips from 1977 made me realise why Punk and New Wave music caused such a stir in the late 70s. You can see that *Top of the Pops* was done in a certain way... All kind of benign and nicey nicey. A certain kinda look, a certain way of dancing, a certain tone of voice. Then suddenly this punk group came on. I think it was *The Jam*. They were snarling their song, totally different to what had gone before, it was like their lives depended on it. Really made me sit up. They had this really different attitude, a different language, a different way of approaching things altogether. It was like a parable I reckon. These dudes were not dancing the same way, not singing the same way, they had anger and passion and they cared about their lyrics. You could really see it. Do you know what I mean?'

I think, nod a little. Ben goes on.

'They seemed tired of the old ways and they were out there to make something different happen. And when I compared the two styles it seemed so obvious why this new attitude was so completely revolutionary. It was just so anti what everyone else was doing. You had these old rockers pretending to dance and these singers in jumpers sitting at shiny pianos, and up against that these young guns come on with their attitude and their pumping guitars and their lyrics about injustice and complacency. And you know what? That's what I reckon the wilderness is all about. People think of it as time out, some "me-time".' He frames this last phrase in speech marks. 'But it isn't that at all. That's just like, consumer-faith. Jesus was onto something else. He was in a state of change, he was moving from being the local builder-carpenter who could fix your house and mend that table, to being a radical teacher who would shake the world to its very core. A punk rabbi if you like.' He laughs at his own joke. 'Yea, a punk rabbi. Do you see that? He was not going to dance, sing, act or speak in the same way anyone else ever had before, and that took a lot of prep. He was changing out there in his desert, facing himself, sorting out his priorities, getting well-grounded. He was about to make something different happen. A new wave kind of challenge to the way people lived, a punk explosion to their understanding of life. A different attitude, different language, a different way of being entirely. Passion, anger and energy. Something very new was coming about in that wilderness. Like a shocking surge of sound from a pumping punk guitar, Jesus was about to upend the long held perspectives on life.'

I don't know what to say. I'm not sure what to make of a monk who tells parables about *Top of the Pops*. And I'm not sure why he's telling me this now.

'Sounds deep,' I say.

'Is it? I don't think it is. You see to call it 'deep' pushes it away, like it's beyond us, unreachable, okay for some saint in a stained glass window. This is not deep. It's just real. And the punks didn't care because they had so little to lose. Until that time came along they were never gonna be rock stars. They couldn't play disco or ballads or prog rock. And they didn't want to. If they couldn't do punk then they weren't doing anything. And I reckon Jesus was the same. He had to do this punk rabbi thing, because he wasn't going to do anything else. Anything else wasn't real.'

'Is this why you became a monk?'

He shrugs. 'Maybe. No idea, only thought of all this last night. But I knew you'd get it. I knew you'd see what I mean. You do don't you?'

Well... yes... and no. But I just tell him the yes bit.

He's still talking so I try and tune back in.

'People would prefer to soften the blow by mixing the old and the new together. They try and merge rather than replace. But playing two songs at the same time... doesn't really work. Two sounds playing over each other just makes a strange jangle that's confusing and overwhelming.'

'What's this about?' I stop walking and face him. He's unnerving me. 'What are you telling me to do?'

'I'm just telling you about Jesus,' he said, a sadness in his voice, 'when you follow him you become part of him.'

'So?'

'Okay, I don't really know why I'm saying this, just thoughts that came into my head when I was praying for you.'

Brother Ben's been praying for me?

'You can't play two tunes at the same time,' he says. 'If you're listening to The Giggheads you don't want Frank Sinatra crooning in the background, do you? Nothing wrong with either, but you have to let go of one. Jesus commented on that kind of thing, you know, I was reading it last night. He didn't use music he used wineskins and clothes as examples. He said, "It's a strange and unsettling mix that often makes a mess. People prefer the old to the new, and trying to put the two together can cause accidents." '

Ben stops, gives a shrug. He's suddenly run out of words.

'Sermon over,' he says with a grin.

He pats me on the shoulder and wanders off. Brother Ben prayed for me. Wow.

Day 16: Blasphemous Rumours

He prays for a while, standing with his face raised to the sky, eyes open. There is nothing up there. One or two clouds pass by but that is it. He recites the Shema. 'Hear, O Israel! The LORD our God is one. And you must love the Lord your God with all your heart, all your soul, and all your strength. And you must commit yourselves wholeheartedly to these commands I am giving you today... Tell your children...Tie them to your hands as a reminder, and wear them on your forehead. Write them on the doorposts of your house and on your gates...'

There are no gates or doors here. Or children. Nothing to write on or tie to his hands. He prays again. Then waits. Silence. Nothing. Nothing. His mind jumps back to that day at the Jordan, the thunder in the sky, the dove, the voice of his cousin, God so tangible you could press your finger against him. Now he raises his thumb and blots out the sun. He is alone. He prays again, reciting psalm 22. 'My God, my God! Why have you forsaken me? Why do you remain so distant? Why do you ignore my cries for help? Every day I call to you, my God, but you do not answer. Every night you hear my voice, but I find no relief. Yet you are holy. The praises of Israel surround your throne. Our ancestors trusted in you, and you rescued them. You heard their cries for help and saved them. They put their trust in you and were never disappointed.'

He pictures Joseph, alone in prison night after night. Ruth lying awake with her mother-in-law, wondering where their next meal will come from. Esther facing the fact that she may die tomorrow for treason. Job hunched up with his sickness and grief. So many people and their troubles. So many who looked up at this sky and wondered.

'My God, my God... why...'

- - - - - - - - - -

It is always the same with Brother Aidan. He looks as murderous as death whenever I roll up at his study, always barks the same 'Come' whenever I knock, but always waits just long enough until I've raised my fist a second time to rap on the wood again before responding. He always looks at me with suspicion when I shuffle in, but the moment I pull out the old brown notebook and mention one of the saints he is a changed man. Smile, light, chat. He's away. I ask him today if he is named after St Aidan.

'Of course,' he says, jumping up as he says it. 'Of course. Of course. Who else? We all take saints names when we come here.' He circles my chair again. 'Basil the Great, St Benedict of Nursia.'

'St Benedict?'

'Of course. Brother Ben. Patron saint of students. Perfect for a restless young man in training. Brothers Patrick, Jerome, Brendon, Cuthbert, Wilfred. They're all named for the great heroes. Did you know by the way that Aidan founded Lindisfarne?'

'The band?'

He laughs. There is something strange and reassuring about discovering that this tough, ancient monk has heard of pop music.

'The Abbey. At Lindisfarne. After which I believe the band was named. Finger of fudge?'

'Sorry?'

He shoots to his desk and springs open a drawer. Then he holds up two chocolate bars in orange wrappers.

'A finger of fudge,' he says and he flips it across the desk at me. I catch it awkwardly, flinching and clutching it to my chest with both hands, causing the chair to creak for England.

'Aidan came from Iona to England... you know he used to walk from village to village, meeting people on the way and patiently talking with them and meeting them on their level. The king gave him a horse so he wouldn't have to walk, but he gave the horse to a beggar. He wanted to go slow, he wanted to bump into people and chat with them. He wanted to rub shoulders, not peer down his nose...'

Once again Brother Aidan shoots from the hip and I do my best to keep up. When there is a lull and I fear he may be about to return to his curmudgeonly self I say,

'Brother Aidan, Why do you love the old saints?'

Brother Aidan thinks, then, 'Because they are like the giants of mythology, the men who inhabited a different time, a different way of being. And we are inextricably linked to them. We may or may not have faith today but the heroes of old shaped the place we find ourselves in now. They gave us the gift of choice. They left so many landmarks so that we can navigate our way back to God.'

'But so many people say that's outdated now.'

Aidan looks as if he might explode.

'Why? Because you can make a ready meal in two minutes? Because you can flick through a thousand channels on a box in the corner of the room? Does that qualify us to argue with men like Columba and Finian and Cuthbert?' He warms to his task. 'Let me tell you – this wonderful new atheism as they describe it, it's a novelty act! History is overcrowded with millions of believers. Littered with those for whom simple faith was everything. The endless crowds of the faithful who have died for that faith. It may seem naïve to our contemporary minds, but that's because humility is not popular. Arrogance is. Atheism will always be in the minority. Always. And...' he lowers his voice now to a whisper so that I have to strain to hear him, 'I cannot understand the attraction of an ideology which defines itself by what a person does not believe.'

I go looking for Brother Basil. He is in the vegetable garden moving things about. I ask him what he thinks of the glorious new atheism. If he is threatened at all.

'People have always been angry about God,' he says. 'Life is unfair. If there is a God then they want him to tidy it up for them. Either God exists and will make life one long party for us or he doesn't and that's why the terrible things happen. This is the biggest struggle for us regarding faith – to not begin with the premise that the existence of God is all about me getting what I want. The writers of the Bible are clear on this. Life is difficult and we must wrestle with it, but as we wrestle so we are searching for God's way. It's the nature of free will. None of us wants to be a pawn in a divine chess match, do we? We want the freedom to choose how we act. It's God's great gift to us. But we cannot then demand that God keep removing that freedom of choice if some people choose evil over good. We cannot demand that God suddenly turn life into that chess game and us into pawns when the going gets terrible.'

'Does that mean you are or you are not threatened by atheism?'

'It means I am as much as anyone else. When the awful things happen and I feel powerless and God seems silent then atheism knocks at my door again. But that is faith. Faith is not about answers or proof. Faith is a most particular kind of commodity. We are asked to place it in a God who was and is before everything. A God outside of time, outside of the questions. The word 'God' is an inflammatory one to a lot of people, they don't just hear the name of the creator, they hear all those things that have gone wrong in their life and all those times when God seemed absent or impotent. When he appeared to be unwilling or unable to do anything about it. And that's what they react to. At the end of the day many people have genuine issues about God but are not able to voice the questions they really have tucked away in the back of their minds. To hear those you have to tune in carefully. Very carefully. A man who hates God because there is a war in Asia and children dying of starvation in Africa is most likely more upset about the loss of his cousin, or the father who neglected him when he was little.'

He lifts a tiny carrot and the expression on his face moves from a sombre setting to a bright one.

'Look at that! How did that happen? Wrong time of year, and we don't plant carrots here. It's amazing what grows sometimes.'

Day 17: Another Day In Paradise

'As the dear longs for the water in the desert... as a working man dreams of a cold beer on a hot day... as a spurned lover aches for comfort and the mending of that broken heart... as a dying child pleads for a bowl of rice. So our souls long for you. Our deepest being cries out, screams, shouts, roars for that thing which seems so out of reach.'
Up The Creek Having Burnt The Paddle by Pew Hadovood

- - - - - - - - - - -

I've been sitting in the battered old armchair in my shed flicking through Dickens since four. *A Christmas Carol*. The weather has thrown in a retro blast of temporary winter. Couldn't sleep because of the cold so I went to the big house and stole a red hot shower. When I say flicking through Dickens, scrolling is probably more accurate with an e-reader. It's a clever tale, which of course is patronising, but I think it is. A ghost story which is really about social injustice. If only I'd written it. Mind you, if I had I'd have been dead for a century or more, so I don't mind too much. But it's a great idea. I always thought of *A Christmas Carol* as a cosy story for the festive season with a few ghosts and some goodwill thrown in. Which it is, but of course, it's something much more. Charlie D was attempting to dredge up a whole load of other things too. As he always was with his gripping yarns. He had an impoverished background and was constantly revisiting the sadness and troubles of the poor in his books. It's said that he went and read to the downtrodden out there in the streets. And more than that, he supported the ragged schools for poor children and worked hard to highlight the problem.

I used to think that being a Christian was mostly about me getting my sins forgiven and being allowed into heaven when I die. Now I'm not so sure, it seems that huge swathes of the Bible are dedicated to what it means to light up the world for God. And that's where the parables come in. Most of them are not about getting into heaven, they are about how to live on earth. I jump from Dickens's Christmas to Matthew's Jesus.

'You are the preservative in the world, the e-numbers,' says the man from Nazareth. 'Keep a preservative in its packet and it'll never do any good. The food it was meant for will go bad. Keep it tidily sealed in the cupboard and the rest of the food may well start to stink. Badly. Leave it long enough and your cupboard will be doing a good impression of a blocked toilet after a night in a curry house. Pretty soon the stench escapes and pervades the kitchen like a bunch of invisible convicts who snuck out through the prison sewer, then the whole house gets overrun and the neighbourhood starts to go downhill. Maggots appear and multiply like little tubular flesh-eating monsters, rats the size of dogs start eating their way through the walls and carpets. House prices drop and a mob surrounds your home bearing torches and pitchforks. The army is called out and the street is cordoned off...'
A cautionary tale. A cartoon worthy of a place in one of the papers.

Preservatives were made to be added to everything to stop this kind of corrosion explosion; a little influence mixed in to enhance the whole dish. Preservatives aren't much to look at, you wouldn't put them in a dress and send them down a catwalk for the front cover of *Vogue*, but when they get working they do a unique job, they bring health and benefit, and magnify the flavour no end.

God's people were invited to be different, to mirror their God who was different. Other people would then see that and want to get in on the action. Instead the people of God polished their BC light bulbs and patted themselves on the back, glorying in their wonderful 'chosen' status, even using that as an excuse to avoid the other nations and thereby push them away from God. Jesus shook his people rigid.
    'Do the world some good' he said, 'you've been chosen by God to light up the planet. Get out there and spark up.'
Like I said, all this is gut-wrenching for someone like me who would rather have a cushy Christianity which doesn't demand a whole lot and just makes me feel better about myself.

And this is why the likes of Brother Aidan and Brother Basil impress me so much. Brother Aidan may be fierce but he's a fierce hero in my book. These men have dedicated themselves to God in a way that is wholehearted. I couldn't do it, but then maybe that's the point. They can, they are the right shape for this. I don't mean it's easy for them. Not at all. But I'm not them. It's easy to look at someone else and tell them how they should honour God. It's the easiest thing in Christendom. But loving the Lord my God with all my heart, soul, mind and strength means I have to search out who God is and who I am and then do it in my way. With my own mind, heart, soul and strength. Someone else's plans won't work.

Sounds good, I just have to apply it then. All this self-sermonising is making me thirsty. I stick on the kettle.

There's a knock on the door. It's Brother Aidan. He never comes to my shed. He looks as if he turned up his fierce face setting to eleven.
    'Did you take a shower this morning?'
I admit I did.
    'Well don't! Not at that time.'
    'But I...'
    'You need to think young man,' he jabs his temple, 'think!'
I do think. I think about killing Brother Aidan. He frowns a frown of death at me and then he is gone. He didn't say much but I am seriously deflated. I guess I disturbed his sleep. Or his praying. I try to remind myself that he's a fierce hero again. But right now he just seems fierce. Didn't Jesus tell us be nice and love each other? It's unfair. I was just cold. Stupid monastery.

Day 18: Invisible Touch

He trips over the rock. Didn't see it coming. Turns and stares it down, as if they're about to have a gunfight. Slingshots at dawn. His foot throbs a little, he reaches into his sandal and rubs the sole. He has lifted a few of these beauties in his time. Good solid rocks for the corners. You need the best for the foundations. Need a good eye to spot them too. He places his foot on the rock. Sizes it up. One day he'll be like that. The first stone in a new building. Not perhaps the rock they all expect, not the kind of building they want either. 'The Messiah will cleanse the land and re-establish the temple,' they all say. Well, he will and he won't. There'll be a new construction all right, but it won't be made out of inanimate, solid stuff. It'll be the opposite, a living, breathing, arguing, questioning kind of temple. A bunch of pilgrims struggling to make something together. Like a human pyramid constantly on the verge of collapse. And the cornerstone, the foundation rock? Plenty will do what he just did. Miss it and trip and angrily dismiss it. It won't be the right shape, the right shade, or consistency for them. They'll dismiss it, they'll dismiss him, out of hand. But he'll still be there. And some will realise what's going on. While others fall sprawling, their faces in the dirt, others will take up the challenge and start building. Wise builders and foolish builders. There could be a good story in that.

- - - - - - - - - -

The reading in chapel this morning is about Hannah being desperate for a baby. Hannah, Sarah, Rachel, Elizabeth, Samson's mum. So many childless women in the Bible, the book's full of them. Their stories diverge from mine though. Take a different route through the maze of family life. They end up with a baby.
I stroll out deep in thought and walk straight into a cloud. There's a heavy mist again this morning, God's cloud is back. That pillar hanging in the desert.

Basil catches me by the arm before I can walk too far.

He asks me about the baby again. No prizes for guessing why. We walk into the empty quad and I tell him about my guilt.

'I wonder if I left it too long. I kept putting it off you see. She wanted a baby for a while and if I'd not wasted time maybe it wouldn't have been about trying to rescue our marriage and maybe we wouldn't have had a baby that was gonna die. But I was scared. I didn't want the commitment, didn't want to be tied down. Now all that seems... weak... fickle... why did I put it off?'

'The why questions are the frustrating ones,' Brother Basil says. 'The why questions to be honest are blind alleys. If I knew why my wife had died so young do you think it would make up for my loss? I have to be honest. I don't. The answer to the why question wouldn't dry any tears for me. It really wouldn't.'

'Your wife died?'

He smiles a wistful smile. 'It was a long time ago now.'

'Did you have children?'

He shook his head. 'We never had time. Fell in love, had a short year together and she was gone. I still think about her most days.'

'I'm sorry.'

He nods. 'You never know what's behind the mask eh?' he says with a chuckle. 'No one ever expects a monk to be a grieving widower.'

We walk in silence for a while. Brother Basil seems easy with that. I'm constantly trying to work out what to say next.

'We light our candles and others blow them out again,' he says suddenly.

'What?'

'I often think about that, our little symbols of faith. I've seen so many candles over the years, people sending up their grief and their longings and the loss to God. Just a match-head placed against a tiny wick. It's nothing is it? Burns for a short time then it's gone. How can that mean anything at all? Before long I or Brother Pat or Brother Fin come along and blow them out. Gone.'

'You don't mean that?' I say. 'You can't mean that.'

He looks at me sternly for a second then the smile cracks across his face. 'Of course not. But on the face of it that's all faith is, a connected series of symbols and actions and coincidences. I see you light a candle and that's that, just a bit of extra work for me to blow it out and clean up the wax. But to you it's a lost child, a lost marriage, a lost job. A quest for a future. That's what so much of faith is. We follow an invisible God with all our hopes and pain and dashed plans, and we join in with him. Reach into his invisible world for a brief moment.'

'I wish he wasn't invisible,' I say with a certain amount of feeling.

'Yes. We don't do well with the invisible God, do we. We want something concrete, which is why we make statues and crosses and buildings. Something we can see to put our hope in. But you see this...' He waves his hand around. I see nothing.

'This,' he repeats, pointing off.

'There's nothing, just the...'

'Exactly. Just the mist. The pillar of cloud. The best symbol of the invisible God. Can't box it or measure it, or pin it down or nail it to a church noticeboard. The pillar of cloud. Or even better, Jesus's picture – God is like a gust of wind. That's what he told Nicodemus. God is like the breeze, and you cannot control him. Or see him. I suppose if he was visible it might mean a waiting list for an interview, or worse still, having to phone up and leave a message with an automated answering service.' He chuckles. 'That would never do.'

'Is that what prayer is?' I ask him. 'Reaching into the invisible world.'

'I suppose so, it's many things. Reaching in and bringing some of it back with us. That's really important, bringing some of God's world into this one. His justice, kindness, humour, laughter, hope, courage, patience. It's like we put our weak fist through the wall of this world and take a fragile hold on something good on the other side. But it's more than that. It's nourishment for us.'

'And what about when we pray for others?'

'I'm no expert,' says Brother Basil, though I'm sure he's lying, 'prayer is a little like a window. We look through it into this other world. We strain to see God's perspective, and we tap on the glass to see if we can get his attention.'

'Do you think he answers prayers?'

'All the time, but not in the prescribed way people often talk about. I think he hears all kinds of pleas and longings from all kinds of people and often some kind of 'coincidence' appears to happen. But I fight any system which turns God into a vending machine where you just push the right buttons to get the results you want. I think that's almost counter to what it means to follow the invisible God. It turns him into a machine instead of a caring, creative, independent being. I understand that we'd all like to control him, you'd like a second stab at your marriage, so would I. But as painful as it is, and believe me I know it's painful, we have to let him be God on those kind of things. Remember Jesus's little prophecy about the problem of being human – 'In this world you will have trouble.' He smiles again, but there's a little sadness about it, 'and if I sound a little too tidy on this subject feel free to thump me.'

We walk back in silence but this time I don't worry about having nothing to say, we both seem at ease with the lack of words. And I don't thump him either. Before we separate he stops me, pulls me back by the arm.

'You know the most important thing about prayer is that we're not asked to be experts. We none of us get very good at it. But that's not the point. We're just invited to do it.'

Day 19: Nineteenth Nervous Breakdown

He thinks on Hezekiah. And Moses. And the bronze snake that linked them. That snake had travelled. Down the ages, through the years. Began life in the wilderness. The people walk into a whole nest of trouble and get bitten by snakes. So they need healing, what to do?

'Quick, make a model of the same kind of snake, but a benign one, one that won't kill them but will save them. Stick it on a pole and lift it up and invite everyone to look to God by looking to that symbol.'

'Really? A model of the very thing that's killing us?'

'Sure. Find healing by looking in an unexpected place.'

'But God said don't make an idol.'

'Ah but this is not an idol. This is a signpost. This is the means to finding your way to the living God.'

So they look. Some of them. And they get healed. One day soon Jesus will find himself like that, held up, a symbol of the very thing that is killing the people. And the invitation will come again, look to that symbol, that place of oppression and hopelessness and criminality. Look to that and find healing. Others will laugh, or turn it into their own kind of glamorous image, but you look to it and find the living God, right here at work, busy on the earth.

Incredible to think that Moses's bronze snake was still around in King Hezekiah's day. But it was. Centuries later and the healing symbol, the sign of God's presence, the little arrow pointing the way towards the healing creator, the big man's logo, had morphed into something else. It had become a god itself. Look to the snake, worship the snake, bow down to the snake that Moses made. It must be precious because our forefathers created it, and it's an antique, and people have used it for centuries, it's a miracle it has survived when so much else has been lost. So it must be of God. The snake is precious, the snake is divine. No it's not, says Hezekiah, it's getting in the way. The symbol that was designed to lead people to God is leading them away. The snake has become a distraction, and worse, a corrupting thing. Smash the snake, destroy it. Take a hammer and let the sound of the blows be heard in the land. Once the making of the snake brought life, now the breaking of it will do the same. The people will lose their idol and find their God. Smash it up, now. Let's start again.

Will they do that with him? Turn the signposts into something else. Make them too precious, too powerful. Make idols out of the symbols of God and start to forget the real things of God. The things he is getting in shape for out here in the desert. Will the people argue about metal and wood and rules and regulations, all the while forgetting humility and compassion and patience and sacrifice? He can see it may happen. It has always been the way with people. The default option is to get your wires crossed. He must face this, he is going to take a good look at the world.

- - - - - - - - - - -

Someone's playing music. I can hear the distinct sound of percussion in tiny headphones. It's 7.30am. I grab my jeans, pull on my hoodie and reach for the door. It's misty outside, the place has a glow on it like some old Vincent Price horror movie. The tinny drumming gets louder. I recognise the track, an old one by Aztec Camera. *Good Morning Britain.* Appropriate lyrics but the pumping wall of sound is not what everyone wants to wake up to. I narrow my eyes and squint into the haze. There's a figure out there, don't think it's Vincent Price, but you never know round here. A tall spectre turns and sees me, too late I've been rumbled, whatever zombie is up at this time of day is coming for me. I stand my ground. Maybe it's one of the two guys who've come to change church. At this time of day with nothing but gloom around I sincerely hope it's the taller one and not the one doing a good thug impression. The figure comes closer. It smiles at me. The music grows louder as he pulls his earphones off the sides of his head.

'Hi!' he says, 'sorry, did I wake you.'
It's Brother Ben. In jeans and a huge jumper. With an old comic in one hand and an iPod in the other.

'I wasn't sure which cabin they put you in, The Shack or The Cooler,' he says.

'Which one's this?'

'The Shack. We call it that 'cause people seem to bump into God there. I don't think he does any cooking for them though.'

'Why The Cooler?'

Brother Ben laughs. 'Why d'you think – it's as cold as Ann Robinson's heart in there. The other two guys must be in it, we're obviously testing their mettle.'

I ask him about his outfit. The lack of habit. He bats at a fly with his comic, it's a copy of The Beano, and he scores a direct hit. The black insect zings like a rock past my ear, buzzing as it goes. He raises a triumphant fist and grins.

'Day off,' he says. 'Best kept secret. Monks get time out now. Don't suppose you got any coffee on the go? Could murder a strong one right now.'

He presses the stop button on his iPod and we slip inside. Embarrassed I make quick efforts to clear up a bit. He waves a hand.

'Don't worry about that, mate. You should see my cell. Compared to the carnage in my place this pad looks like a bomb missed it.'

'You're up early for a day off,' I say and he nods.

'Never did get in the habit of sleeping in much and normally we'd have to be up for prayers real early, so I'm out of whack when it comes to lolling about in bed. I'm happy just wandering about listening to my iPod and getting some space.'

'What's a monk do on his day off?'

'FAQ,' he says.

'Pardon?'

'Frequently asked question,' he says and takes the coffee I hand him. I sip mine, it's very strong and for the first taste of the day nearly melts the roof of my mouth. 'Ah perfect,' he says, 'was just thinking out there how much I needed some of this. What did you ask? Oh yea, days off, some don't really take one, the old school guys, been around since the time when no one had any time out. Me, I just wander about, sometimes walk into the village, take my comic and my iPod. Find a pub or a tree with a good view depending on the time of year.'

This is not what I expected.

'Yea,' he says, 'disappointing eh? You probably expected us to sit in front of oil lamps translating ancient Mayan manuscripts and brewing dandelion wine all day. I think it was once like that. In fact, monks were once the chief brewers of England. Not now. Sadly.' He pauses and drinks. 'Still a challenge though. Not exactly muscular Christianity, but it's not a night at the multiplex either. Hey, do you have any grub?'

I pull out my latest packet of Bourbon biscuits. 'These or cornflakes?' I say.

'Genius!' he says and tucks in to the Bourbons.

Brother Ben can eat. I discover that. He's tall but lanky as hell. Not sure where all the food goes really. Can't help wondering if they feed him enough in a monastery but then maybe he gets all that leftover cabbage soup some days. Lovely.

Brother Ben stays around for a while. We wander outside and climb a couple of moorland hills. I crack out some Cheddars for a post-breakfast snack. I ask him if he's ever worked in a cinema.

'No but that sounds cool!' he says, eyes wide. 'Wall-to-wall movies.'

'Wall-to-wall popcorn too. You know what? Kids buy a huge tub of the stuff then sit on the front row and kick it so that it fans out for half a mile. That ain't very cool if you're the guy with the brush and shovel.'

'Ouch, sounds like you and the cinema got some history.'

'I worked in a multiplex and I'm scared I'll end up back there.'

He rubs his chin. 'I guess it's okay if you're waiting to go to college or something.'

Exactly. If you're lost in your own life it's terrifying.

'D'you ever see the movie *American Beauty*?' I ask him.

'I think so, some guy films a plastic bag.'

I laugh. 'Yes, and Kevin Spacey has a mid-life crisis, packs in his job and goes to work in a burger bar. In the movie he has a great time doing that. But life isn't the movies. I didn't have a great time when I ended up behind a hot dog counter.'

'You know my favourite movie? *Regarding Henry*. It's an old film, really old, goes way, way back, made in the early 90s I think. Harrison Ford has a breakdown after being a tough lawyer. Can't do his job anymore. A mate who's a nurse comes round and tells him that he once had breakdown and it changed his life. Inspired him to become a nurse and help people like Henry. Great scene. Really cool scene. He tells

Henry 'don't listen to anyone trying to tell you who you are, it may take some time but you'll figure yourself out.' You know what the Bible says in proverbs? I love proverbs. Weird, funny, sensible kind of book. It says, 'Sometimes it takes a bad experience to make us change our ways.' Obvious, but kind of profound too.'

He looks me straight in the eye, bats me on the arm with his rolled up comic and says nothing more. We amble back to my shed and then he wanders off and I remember something I heard not long back in a sermon.

'Other people told me to invite Jesus into my life, they never warned me that if I did, he'd bring other people with him. Jesus never seems to come alone.'

I'm sitting there thinking about this, half-praying, half-distracted, when there's a knock at the door.

It's Bill again, Steve's mate, half of the two-man, world-changing combo. That's frustrating. I was just getting into the mood to break bread with my tea and biscuits. It keeps happening, I try to have a quiet moment remembering Jesus and other people keep breaking in.

  'Want a cuppa I ask?' as he hovers on the doorstep.

He doesn't answer, just sways a little. It's only 10.45am but I have a feeling something stronger than PG Tips has crossed his lips already. He nods, over-enthusiastically. He comes in. I let him have the old armchair and I settle on the side of the bed. He doesn't have a mug with him so I let him have mine and I re-use a paper cup that's been holding my toothbrush. Doesn't taste great.

  'I'm doing the remembering bit,' I say, waving my packet of Bourbon biscuits at him.

  'Remembering?'

  'Jesus. "Eat and drink and remember me".'

He thinks for a moment and stares at my Bourbons. Suddenly his eyes widen, you can almost hear the penny drop.

  'You mean... you can use biscuits?'

I nod. 'And tea. Why not? Eat and drink he said. Any food can remind you that you need Jesus in your being – the way you need food and water.'

'Jesus in me?' he thinks again. Another wide-eye moment, another light bulb goes on in his head.

'That's why we do it... because food goes in... Jesus goes in... and makes us strong?'

'Yup, and satisfied. And nourished. And fuelled up to do something.'
We eat biscuits for a while and sup tea.

'I like that,' he says. 'I like that because it feels different, because it's not bread and wine in a church. Feels right.'

'Can't survive without food, can't survive without the son of man.'
He frowns.

'Jesus,' I clarify. 'The son of man. It's a description he nicked from the book of Daniel.'
Silence. Then,

'I can't do it,' Bill suddenly says. 'I'm a fake.'
I laugh. 'Join the club.'
But I shouldn't have, I shouldn't have laughed. He's serious. And more than serious. He's depressed and drunk about it. His face is as tense as a world cup penalty shoot-out.

'I thought you were all for changing the world,' I said.
He snorted. 'I wanna, but the past keeps catching up with me. Won't let me go. Can't do what I should do.'

'That reminds me of someone. St Paul? Ever heard of him?'
I grab my leather Bible and flick to Romans 7. I read him a bit. 'I know I am rotten through and through so far as my old sinful nature is concerned. No matter which way I turn, I can't make myself do right. I want to, but I can't. When I want to do good, I don't. And when I try not to do wrong, I do it anyway.'

'Yes,' he jabs a stub of a finger at me, 'yes! That's me. Exactly. Can't do it. Can't be a Christian. May as well give up. Just a mess. Hopeless case.'

'Maybe we're all hopeless cases.'

'What?'

'Well if you can't do it and St Paul can't, and I know I can't... then we're all frappuccinoed aren't we?'
He frowns again. Can't make this out.

'But you make it sound like we're all failures,' he says.

'Aren't we?'

'I'm not!' Bill's clearly indignant about this. 'I've been set free from all that.'

'But you just told me you couldn't do it.'

'I can't. But I'm still a triumphant Christian, reigning in heavenly places. Steve told me.'

'There's nothing wrong with being a mess you know,' I say.

'Jesus didn't die for losers and wasters.'

Well… 'Actually he did. That's the point, Bill.'

Bill doesn't like this. He stands and walks about.

'It's not the point! It's not fair. It's too hard. Too hard to be a Christian. Too damn xxxxxxx hard.'

'I agree, you're wearing me out.'

'But it's not supposed to be hard. I can do all things through Christ who strengthens me.'

'Said the man who wrote Romans 7 and admitted he was a bit of a loser and a waster.'

'You can't say that about St Paul!'

'I think I just did. Listen Bill. I'm not trying to be difficult. I promise. But I'm done with all that successful Christian living. I know what I'm like, and God knows too. And St Paul said, "Thank God for Jesus 'cause he gets us through all the trouble and hypocrisy and inability to live the Christian life." Take that to heart mate. Otherwise you'll wear yourself out trying to be good all the time.'

Bill looks at me long and hard. Then he burps. It don't smell great.

'And go and have a good walk or a lie down, or maybe both. Find a field and crash out.'

He goes. I collapse on the bed.

Day 20: Hungry Like The Wolf

The hunger. It drives him on now. It's the third phase. The first was the usual 'When's lunch?' kind of pangs, eventually passing into the kind of 'I'm not hungry anymore' phase. But this is different. This is head-swimming weakness. He's disorientated, the rocks float a little, hovering like manna shimmying down from above. Images from the past creep out of the shadows of his psyche. Kids he played with walk by him in a trance. Women, friends of his mother's, come out of suddenly-appearing houses to scold him or offer him food. There's an old widow down the street hunting high and low for a lost coin. A farmer races by yelling and hollering after his escaping sheep. Young men wander past seeking adventure, prodigals like himself, out looking for some action. They all look lean and mean and hungry. Suddenly the desert is alive, full of people, his solitude is shattered. Lack of food has brought the world to his doorstep.

The temple suddenly looms before him. Where did that come from? He trudges through the colonnaded walkway, passing a figure surrounded by religious teachers and scribes. Something's going on. Brows are furrowed and quizzical looks exchanged. What's happening? He stops, listens, nods, smiles. He remembers. That temple visit. The animated speaker is just a boy, and the boy is in full flow, his eyes wide, his mouth working, his fingers jabbing the air. He is in his element and the others wonder how he does it. He should be out of his depth here, but he looks more at home than the bushy eye-browed, saggy-jowled experts. They can barely get a word in edgeways, the odd question here, the occasional comeback there. But the boy flurries on, stories and questions and witty comments spilling from his lips like water from a freshly discovered spring. He smiles again, walks on, he doesn't need to listen. He's not arrogant. He just knows those stories. He told them. It's good to be reminded of them though. They will come in handy soon. The tenants, the fish, the buried treasure, the virgins, the wedding, the talents... He'll come back to them soon enough. He walks on. His head is clearing again, the stranglehold of the hunger receding. He knows where he is going now. Up to the temple pinnacle. He has an appointment up there.

- - - - - - - - - - -

I drop a little too hard on the rock beside this lake and the jutting surface thumps my rump. I'm not hungry like Jesus is hungry. I'm not famished. Not starving. But I am trying to go without breakfast. Breakfast! Jesus went forty days without so much as a cream cracker. I'm just skipping cornflakes. I pull my Bible from my rucksack and flip to Isaiah. Where's that chapter again, that little verse I found earlier this morning? Ah yes, chapter 25, verse 6. God providing for his people. A big feast. Lashings of Yorkshire pudding, roast beef, leeks and gravy. And roast potatoes. Mountains of them. God will feed his people, but alone in the wilderness he refuses to feed himself. Jesus knows Isaiah well, he knows now that one day he will feed his people, two days in fact, and some of them may spot the reference. But not today, today he's feeding no one. Not even himself.

He must have been sorely tempted to turn those rocks into bread... Sorely, sorely, sorely. Desperately. Maybe day after day after day after day. We read it just the once. And then just once a year. Jesus lived it every stomach-groaning morning. Every second of hunger and agony. Every time he woke up and had the power to magic up a banquet. Whatever the first century equivalent of bacon, eggs, sausages, tomatoes, fried bread, black pudding and mushrooms is. I shift on the hard rock that's serving as my seat. It would make a good sized loaf. Freshly baked and still steaming. The smell somehow fills my nostrils and for a moment I'm back home in our local cake shop. All hot loaves and cool custard tarts. Ah those custard tarts. And that makes me wonder. Would I do the custard tarts? Would I? Would I? I'm not sure. If I could... what would I really make? I'd do something else, of course I would. And I know what. Doughnuts. I'd be tempted to turn them into custard doughnuts... with chocolate on top. *Tempted...* wasn't that a song by the band Squeeze, *Tempted by the fruit of another...* hmm, fits for today all right.

I walk down to the big house, my head suddenly churning with songs about food. *Chocolate Girl, Raspberry Beret, There's a Guy Works Down the Chip Shop Swears He's Elvis, Black Coffee in Bed, Rock Lobster, Red Red Wine, Two Pints of Lager and a Packet of Crisps, Vindaloo, Pulling Mussels From a Shell, Brown Sugar, Blueberry Hill, Honey Honey, Sugar Sugar, Peaches, The Fast Food Song, American Pie, Banana Splits, The Candy Man, The Ketchup Song...* 'When the moon hits your eye like a big piece of pie...' a huge piece of pie more like... massive... Jurassic... bigger than the London eye... steak and mushroom... perfect pastry... cooked in ale... with extra chips and onion rings... 'Food glorious food magical food wonderful food marvellous food fabulous food beautiful food glorious food...'

Custard doughnuts with chocolate icing on top. Can't get them out of my head now. I've come down here to ponder on God and all I'm doing is planning lunch. During the little service in the chapel, whilst monks sing plainsong and incense mingles with the old musty smell of ancient faith, I'm trapped in a culinary quagmire. To break out of this gastronomic trance I flick to Luke. That tussle in the desert, the duel under the sun. Jesus quotes the Old Testament to the devil and it's not what I expect. He uses a quote from that ancient book of Deuteronomy, Moses's leaving speech if you like, his dying wishes to the people. It's in the early chapters, somewhere around eight I think. I riffle pages again, a little too frenetically, others glance up at me. I grimace an apology and move the paper in slow motion. Here it is. 'God humbled you,' says Moses, sweat on his brow and the spit flying from his mouth in tiny droplets as he pushes out the words. 'He humbled you by letting you go hungry and then turning up and feeding you with manna. And why? Why?' Silence. The people don't want to get the answer wrong. 'No one had ever tasted manna before. No one had ever seen manna before. This was God food, bread from the divine breadmaker. Why did he do it? He did it to teach you that people need more than bread for their life; real life comes by feeding on every word of the LORD.'

I sit back in my pew, feel the bruise forming nicely on my backside from my slumping on that rock. This is a little surprising. So… food can lead us to God then. In the wilderness Jesus holds back on eating, but in the desert God fed the people when they were hungry – doing it in a remarkable way so they would know he had been the perpetrator. Right now the only thing lack of food is doing is leading me to dream about my next meal. Three course meals float before my eyes and I swear I can smell curry with a peshwari naan.

Hunger dominates my worldview, and maybe that's the point. It's not bread *or* God – it's bread *and* God. The people are starving and God gives them bread, he doesn't hold back, his provision was designed to remind people they needed him… not unlike the bread and wine at communion, reminding us of God with us. Jesus feeds a crowd with bread and fish because he cares about them, hopes it will lead them to the one who made everything. Then he breaks bread and spills wine, leaves food as the best reminder we can have that God is with us, and we need him like we need meat and doughnuts and curry and custard tarts. This is revolutionary for me, makes my head spin a little, especially after no breakfast. Food is a constant reminder of God. Food is everywhere. At least it is where I come from. I glance over at the communion table. There's a cup of wine and some jagged bits of bread on a silver plate. 'Eat,' says Jesus, 'eat this bread which God gave to the people in the desert, and which I gave to a crowd of thousands, eat it and remember these stories – you will always need food and you will always need the divine breadmaker.' Brilliant. Simple and brilliant. He allowed people to get hungry in the first place so he could then provide for them, to encourage them to look to him for help and provision, to avoid merely becoming self-sufficient. Our need of food reminds us that there is someone who invented it. Hunger leads us to the one who designed us to get hungry, not so we can escape this life, so we can weave him into the normal mundane things that dominate our living.

We need bread and we need God.

'Someone's been playing with my train set.'

I bump into Brother Ben on my way to evening chapel.

'Train set?'

'Yea – it's in the basement.'

'Well... how do you know?'

'Because someone plugged it in and tried switching it on.'

I do my best to look as if I didn't go down in the basement and try switching on his train set. I don't do well at it.

'It was you, wasn't it?' For a moment Ben does a good impression of Brother Aidan. He's a lot taller than Aidan and I'm seriously worried. Then he grins.

'Come down after chapel. I'll show you it properly. It works and everything. I'm supposed to have given it up really, but you know, can't hurt to send a few engines round the track every so often.'

Brother Ben takes me round to the hatch I used the other day. He leads me inside, opens a cupboard in the yellow shadows at the far end of the corridor, flicks a fuse-breaker then comes back and goes into the train-setted room. The moment he flicks the switch there is a humming noise and three engines start to move. One of them crashes into some stationary carriages and he starts linking them up to the engine and replacing them on the track.

'It's a great layout,' I say. 'I had one, but much smaller.'

'My dad built it for me,' he says.

'I envy you.'

He shrugs. 'Well... maybe you shouldn't. It wasn't long before my parents split up. I used to escape into this, imagine myself in this world, hiding from all the shouting and chaos. It kind of brought me to God too. I imagined him driving one of the trains, and some days I'd go on his train 'cause I felt he'd take me somewhere safe and exciting.'

He watches the trains moving round, lost in that world for a while. He absentmindedly adjusts some of the figures and the scenery as we stand there. After a while I say,

'When I was down here the other day I saw a monk with yellow socks. D'you know who it was?'

'Yellow socks?' He thinks then snaps his fingers. 'Could be Brother Horace.'

'Horace?'

'Yea, I know folks have spotted him from time to time.'

'Who is he then?'

'Oh a brother from the 1920s. A really wise dude.'

'No I don't mean who was he named after, I mean who is he? Now.'

'And I told you – a brother from the 1920s, a really wise dude.'

'But age-wise that would make him... oh! You mean...' and I say this very slowly as if Ben is suddenly only five years old, 'there isn't a yellow-socked monk called Horace in these parts nowadays?'

Ben grins and nods. 'Nope.' Pause. We watch the trains again. Then Ben glances across at me, a sly look on his face. 'I suppose you won't want to hang around here much longer then in case he shows up again.'

We get out of there pretty quick. At least... I do.

Day 21: I Can See For Miles

Jesus stands on the high point of the temple mound and looks down. His head spins a little, his foot kicks against some loose dust, a cloud of the stuff spills over the edge. He remembers the words he grew up with, 'God is my refuge, my place of safety, he will rescue me from every trap. Keep me from every fatal disease. His angels watch over me, ready to protect me, ready to stop me striking my feet on rocks.' The problem is he's planning to walk into a trap, a fatal disease brought on by the Roman occupation. He could pray that God will keep him from that, stop any harm coming his way. But that's not the plan is it? A single bead of sweat slips from his hairline and weaves its way down his face. It brushes his lips before dropping to the dust at his feet. His mind is in turmoil. He feels as if he's sweating blood. God will protect him, his angels watch over him. He sways a little as he looks down again, then lifts one foot and lets it hover in the air. Of course the angels will catch him. Of course they will. It's hot up here. He feels the sun on his head, the emptiness in his stomach. He sways again. He's losing his balance. He leans forward and slips over the edge. At least he does in his mind. But another memory sneaks into his head. Another quote. Israelites jammed in the desert. Losing the plot, asking too many questions.
Moses had struck a rock and found water, but only after the people nearly staged a stoning. So Moses named the place 'Argument'. Later he used this as a reminder, 'Don't test your God, trust him,' he said. 'Don't test your God... Don't test...'

Blasphemers were dragged up there, kicking and screaming, their throats clogged and thick with the bile kicked up by the terror of what was coming their way. Hauled up to the highest point of the temple so they could be thrown all the way down again and executed, hurled half dead then bludgeoned with rocks and snarling voices.

Avoid execution. Angels will fly in and save you. He will remember this day, he logs it in his mind. He has a hunch he will need it when he is surrounded by the men who have come to murder him. It will be tempting, more tempting then than now, to call down angels to rescue him, to break his fall, to avoid the coming pain and execution.

Malachi saw a day like today, he knows that well. 'Look!' the ancient prophet had said, 'your rescuer will appear suddenly at the temple.' Well he has appeared and no one has noticed, but another day will come. Another time when they will notice, when he revisits the temple in the style of the prophets Ezekiel and Zechariah. When he rides in from the East on a donkey. The glory of the Lord coming in through that gateway. People will not miss that sign, the streets and hillsides will be stuffed with pilgrims, and they will all know the old prophet's words. 'Hey! Take a look – here comes your king, right there. Look at him – riding on a humble animal.' That will send a message that no one will miss. The poor and grieving, the meek and persecuted, the peacemakers and those who long for justice in the land. And the powerbrokers too. The Sadducees. The men with clout. The men who can manipulate even the mighty Roman Empire for their own ends.

- - - - - - - - - -

Why is it that when you're not trying to go without food you can happily go for days without a meal, but the moment you decide to stop chomping you could eat a horse. I'll have anything right now, anything. Even the food I hate. Marmite, tripe, runner beans, broad beans, cardboard, tree bark, voles, hamsters, other people's children. I'll eat anything. Yet again food has become my worldview, my frame of reference. Anything edible is fair game. And I can't have any of it! Not at least until elevenses – or ten thirties in my book. That's hours away. Hours. How can I last, how can I survive? I'll faint, pass out, be found lying outside my cabin in a pile of skin and bone. I suppose there are worse places to end my days. Just hope they get to me before the wild animals gnaw the wafer thin strips of flesh from my meagre body.

I think about my own cliff edge. When was it, just ten, twelve days ago? I scared myself that day. It scares me now just thinking about it. Was I really so close to throwing myself off that precipice? There were no angels around to catch me if I had done it, but then again, something held me back. Something stopped me long enough until the rain came and distracted me and urged me home to my shed. Thank God for that rain. It may have killed countless in the days of Noah, but it saved my life. Somehow the wreckage piling up in my mind – the baby, the job, the marriage – pushed me to the brink. Now the temptation to do it seems madness. Now I cannot imagine what I was thinking. I'd never jump. Never.

It's lunch time. At last. At last. At last. At last! I am so desperate I could eat a horse. Or a monk. Or a monk on a horse. Anything. Just bring it on with a knife and fork. Even that terrible pea soup they serve here some days. Even that. I hope it isn't that though. Please no. That would surely be unfair after I've been so godly this morning.

It's pea soup. Unnaturally green, unnaturally grainy, unnaturally gloopy. I dip my spoon in. There are places in the world where hungry people would see this as an answer to prayer. I pray and swallow hard before I eat it. I take a huge hunk of bread and even consider adding marmite, even though I fall well into the 50% of the population that passionately does not not not love it.

Lunch is always a silent meal, although that is stretching the point. There is an awful lot of slurping on the pea soup days as men with few teeth do their best to hoover the green, grainy gloop between their lips. Somewhere in the background Brother Aidan is reading from the sequel to *The Beautiful Manifestations of the Mysterious Cloud of Knowledge* probably known as *The Beautiful Manifestations of the Mysterious Cloud of Knowledge 2*. He's doing his best to impart the ancient 14th Century wisdom but is frequently overpowered by the soup hoovering.

There are of course many periods of silence here. I frequently forget to observe them.

On my way back up to my shed I spot Brother Basil in his garden. Feeding the chickens. They don't appear to observe silence either. I decide to quiz him about the quiet.

'Why do you have silence here?' I ask leaning on the fence.

The fence gives way and I nearly fall headlong. There is not much dignity left in me by the time I get upright again. Brother Basil does not seem to notice. He places his fingertips together and presses them to his old lips. He still looks like a teddy bear to me, generally round and jolly in his ancient brown habit.

'Well, traditionally it's to avoid sin. Ever read the book of James in the New Testament? James describes the tongue as a raging forest fire. Begins with a small spark and before you know it, whoosh! The fire travels and it can set your whole being ablaze. It is potentially seen as destructive, sabotaging the whole of life. Which is true when you think of the damage rumour and slander can inflict. James uses the image of hell itself setting your tongue on fire, as if there's a little devil with a gas lighter on a bamboo cane reaching up to ignite unsuspecting gossips. One of the psalms is quoted as a reason too, but I've always thought it's a little odd. David writes about how he has silenced himself to stop from saying anything wrong, but it burns away inside of him until he just has to speak. So, being quiet makes him – as they say – bust a gut.' He laughs at the thought. 'It's honest I suppose. How many of us try to shut up but can't.'

'What do you think?' I ask.

'I would say that in a world of much noise, it's got to be a good thing to have some silence. Deliberate silence, not just the time when the radio breaks down. Or there's a power cut. Intentional quiet. Probably a luxury to a lot of people. Mothers with young children, people who work in shops and factories where there is wall-to-wall music in the background. Trying to find silence must be a bit like trying to see the stars in a city full of light pollution. What do you think?'

What do I think?

'Yes. What about you and silence?'

'It doesn't bother me, I sometimes want to laugh when we're trying to eat lunch and people mime to each other about passing the bread or Marmite. Someone passed a note today, I saw them passing it from hand to hand on the other side of the long refectory table. Watched in wonder. It turned out it was for me! I opened it, half expecting a blackmail note, and scrawled in Marmite across it were the words, 'You don't eat enough.' I laughed then. Brother Aidan gave me one of his assassinating looks. I didn't eat enough today all right - it was pea soup. Extra green today.'

'Ah, yes. Not Brother Fin's best.' Brother Basil paused then said, 'Some monasteries are in silence all the time.'

'I couldn't live without music,' I said.

'Yes you could,' he replied.

'No I couldn't.'

'Oh yes you could.'

And we leave it there before it begins to sound like the local pantomime.

Day 22: Running On Empty

He wakes again. Another day. Like yesterday, only a little more hungry, a little weaker. He walks, reminisces on his recent years in the workshop. Thinks on his father. He misses his father. He hopes he's stood well in the old man's shoes. There were days when the learning wasn't so easy, days they argued and haggled over bits of wood and stone, sawdust on their sweating brows and fingers jabbing at each other. His father was a good man, upright, but not respected. Not really. He might have been had it all turned out differently. Had he not been a fool and decided to stick with Mary and a son that wasn't his own. He could have been a real stand-up guy in the community. But the stories never really went away. A small place remembers. Especially controversy like that. He just hopes many will remember his father differently when he emerges from the desert, see him in a new light when they see the son at work, that boy who wasn't really his, stepping up to the plate and shining a light in some dark places. Maybe then they'll remember Joseph and think differently. 'He did the right thing,' they'll say, 'look how remarkably his son turned out.' He walks on. Another day. A little more sand through the hourglass. He walks, he thinks, same steps as yesterday. He prays for his family. The brothers and sisters and mother left. He knows that it won't be easy for them. He's not stupid. He is about to extend his family and where he comes from that will seem like the worst slur on a widowed mother. He's about to spend more time with other mothers and siblings than with his own. And his own may not appreciate that. He walks on. Another day. A little closer to the new job. Nazareth will need another carpenter-builder now.

- - - - - - - - - - -

Can't help feeling as if I'm drifting. Wake up the same time each morning i.e. dead early. Lie there listening to the sounds of a world away from the city and the traffic. Birds, insects, light rain, gusts of wind, sometimes the odd unidentifiable and occasionally disconcerting sound. But never any roaring cars, or trucks cascading over speed bumps. Never any kids playing football or adults swearing in the street.

I'm not sure if monks swear. Maybe some do when they stub their sandaled toe on the edge of their prayer desk yet again as they clamber up for another early morning trip to the chapel.

What am I doing here? Same quiet routine every day now. Still going to the chapel services, still hear Brother Aidan reading those ancient texts at lunch, still banter with Brother Ben, still break bread with Bourbons and PG Tips each morning. Sometimes alone, sometimes with an unexpected invader...

A football. It bounces off my window nearly cracking the glass. I shoot up out of my seat. Was it really a football, or a blindsided bird not watching where it was going, confused by the space ahead, never heard of glass. Doesn't double-glaze its nest. I glance at the clock, it's only 8.30am. I open the door. There are voices now and the sound of men panting as shoe leather pounds the ground and jabs at a plastic ball. It really is a football. Are you allowed to play football in a monastery? My shed sits a little way out from the main quad and big house, so there is room here for a kick-about and a couple of goals made from jumpers. Or in this case, discarded habits. There are monks out there in jeans and jumpers. Brother Ben and another guy I've seen cooking in the kitchen, Brother Fin I think he's called. They're playing two-a-side, Ben and his mate against Stew the atheist, and real man, world-changer Steve. Bill's there too, he seems to be referee, linesman and ball fetcher. They wave at me to join them (no apology about the slam dunk at my window) so I do the obvious thing and panic. How to get out of this dire situation? I fall back on an age-old trick I once discovered when invited to play pool in a pub... I stare hard at the pitch as if trying to work something out, then slowly shake my head as if I desperately want to but... no... I just can't. It's only half true. I can't. But no way do I desperately want to. I am still haunted by those terrible moments at school when we lined up in the rain along a scuffed white line waiting to not get picked by the school sports heroes; goodlooking, trendy guys who marched up and down beckoning in the direction of us lesser mortals as they formed their team for the coming combat. I was usually about third from last to be picked. Which could have been worse I suppose. Why did they not do that in Maths? Or history? Stick everyone up on a line and get some joker like me to walk up and down selecting the geniuses. Why not? Why not? Why did I never get payback time?

And this is the question I'm left with now, yet again, as I stand watching these more capable sportsmen zigzagging around the scrubland performing some kind of magic with a black and white ball. The stupid thing is I don't really care, but when I get asked to play and yet again have to come up with some fabricated excuse I care very much indeed. It's not about the sport I suppose. It's about looking good, feeling strong, acting like a proper man. A proper man who can kick a ball without looking like a Mr Bean replicant. Thankfully I catch sight of Brother Basil strolling nearby, make a quick gesture of an apology and run for my life.

I ask him how he copes with the routines, the lack of variety and excitement here.

'Routines are good. Order, logic, it can free you up. That's why the services are repetitive. The songs and psalms. There is space to find yourself and lose yourself. Life doesn't have to be all car chases and love affairs.'

'I know that but...'

'It's all those posters. They are everywhere. They are so loud, so vocal. They tell you that life should be glossy, beautiful, engaging and fast moving. Never still. Never quiet. Never...' he looks around. There is the occasional distant sound of the footballers, but no sight of them now or anyone else. 'Empty.'

'Is empty good?'

'Of course. Why must we cram so much into ourselves. It only causes stress and a hundred 'to do' lists. Tasks, pleasure, shopping, achievement, we plan it all and then try and squeeze it into our day. And the more we plan the more we fear stopping the planning. That's what we are here for, so you can throw the 'to do' lists for a while. So you can find stillness, quiet... even emptiness.'

The guys are still playing football, I do my best to sneak past them but they all see me. I flip on the kettle and then get half an idea. I go to the open door and lean on the frame. Watch them for a bit.

'Want any tea and biscuits?' I yell suddenly, surprising myself.

They stop, look at me, look at each other, then Brother Ben grins.

'Cheers!' he yells. 'Be over in a minute!' And he takes the opportunity to kick the ball through an open goal. 'Oh yes!!' he yells with his arms in the air, running around like a mad monk.

I only have one mug and a plastic cup so Ben has his in a waterbottle, Brother Fin sips from the top of an old teapot we find. Bill brings his own heavy duty camping mug, Stew has some kind of utensil that will manipulate into anything from a drinking vessel to a pocket knife. Steve is happy with a gleaming silver flask top. Can't help feeling our mugs are an extension of our manhood somehow. I tell them I break bread every day.

'Really?' asks Steve, 'when?'

I grin. 'Just about now,' I say.

'What?'

Stew laughs. 'He's already doing it,' he says. 'We're all already doing it.'

This sparks confusion at first, then a serious debate about whether it's really what Jesus meant. I could be threatened but I manage to see the funny side. And we sit there, remembering Jesus and arguing about whether this is really acceptable, really the best way. Not unlike a bunch of first century disciples actually.

Find myself thinking that I hope it's okay to see the funny side of breaking bread.

Steve and Bill are off. This is their last day. The world beckons, though it's hard to tell what they feel about it. Bill looks rough. They finish up their tea and go off to throw their things in their bags. Later I catch sight of them through the open door of my shed. I go out, feeling some strange obligation to say goodbye. They look embarrassed. Not quite sure why. Perhaps I shouldn't have come to give them any kind of a send-off, we are blokes after all. Bill looks worried but he smiles and thanks me for 'our chat'. Steve looks perplexed about this.

'Made any plans?' I ask.

Steve says he has, though I get the feeling this is news for Bill. Perhaps Bill doesn't feature in them.

'Keep on doing the guys' stuff,' I say, I think it's important but I'm also glad it's them doing it and not me.

'Oh we will,' says Steve, almost as if it's a threat.

I deliberately give him a big smile and offer my hand. Steve shakes it. Bill grips my shoulder instead. I watch them walk away. Will they change the world? Fill their church, whatever that turns out to be, with wall-to-wall men? When they have gone I go back and look up the bits in the Bible where Jesus meets four fishermen and offers them a new job. Catching men instead of mackerel. Jesus knows how to relate to guys. His stories, his way of life, his leadership style. And when his best mate blows it, he knows how to deal with that too. It's a hard act to follow.

Day 23: Waiting For My Chance To Come

'Forty days is a long time.'
Up The Creek Having Burnt The Paddle by Pew Hadovood

- - - - - - - - - - -

It is a long time. There were times in the past when I longed for days with no pressure, no plans, no demands. Just the freedom to do what I want. Now I have it I'm starting to feel lost. Disorientated. Have time to read but no energy for it. Time to walk, but end up meandering. Time to chat but of course small talk is a foreign land to me, and I'm running out of ideas when I meet people. And the guilt. I'm starting to feel really guilty about having all this time to myself, when so many other people are dragging themselves out of bed to go to dead-end jobs every morning. Or worse. People are waking to days laced with starvation, murder, imprisonment, bereavement, dread. And the guilt is doubled when I think about how I'm not appreciating the time.

Did Jesus wonder if forty days was too long? A waste? Did he think on those folks back home, working hard under terrible Roman oppression. Paying their taxes, scraping a living, wondering about this year's crops. Was he tempted to pack it all in and run back to the workshop, or maybe cut it short by a fortnight? Just do twenty eight days. Was that one of the temptations he faced. 'Go on Jesus, there's nothing more to be gained by hanging around here any longer. You're not doing anyone else any good. Not healing anyone, or showing kindness to anyone. Not changing the world for the better in any way at all. What are you doing here? Just staring at rocks and thinking of your mother's bread. Go home, do something useful with your life. Stop lounging about. This is going nowhere.'

I try to remind myself that the Bible is full of people who were shaped by the waiting around. Joseph and his technicolour coat, which was most likely just brown with impressively large sleeves. He languished in prison for years. Must have wondered why on earth he'd had those dreams of youth. Must have wondered what the images of leadership in his head were all about. Here he is banged up with no future. Okay so he's worked his way up to jail administrator status, but he's still wearing striped pyjamas and eating prison food. Surely his visions were leading to more than this.

Forty days in a monastery hardly measures up to years in jail, though there are times when the walls of my shed seem to start closing in on me. Dreamt a couple of nights ago that my standard issue grey monastic blanket took on a life of its own, grew standard issue arms and started to try and strangle me. We wrestled for the best part of a dream and I woke up exhausted. Surely Christianity isn't supposed to be like this. When I was a newly-converted teenager, fresh out of the womb, I had dreams and visions myself. I was going to climb mountains for God, I was going to change the world, convert my town, be the new Billy Graham and Martin Luther King rolled into one. The world would stand back in awe at my accomplishments for God, all done with the utmost humility, and for no credit of my own.

I get up. No mean achievement on days like this. I look out of the window, the rain is coming down so heavily it's like a car wash out there. I pull on my clothes and go outside. It doesn't take long. I'm wet through in minutes, but somehow it helps. It helps to feel something, to be distracted from my doubts and questions. I think about Noah. He went somewhere for forty days. Must have wondered if it would ever get better again. Get dry. The stench of animal crap must have been overwhelming, would he ever taste sweet air again? Would he ever be able to walk about without putting his foot in camel dung every third step? And what would they do with all these rabbits? He must have wondered if it would stop raining, maybe the world would just be forever wet, the level rising and rising till they were floating outside heaven's door, knock, knock, knocking to get in. Maybe it will never stop raining now. My hair is matted to my head like a swimming cap and the little rivulets of rain run over my eyes. I turn away from my shed, I don't want to go back to that place of the attacking blanket and the besieging walls. I'm going for a walk. Soaked or not I'm going to kid myself I'm travelling somewhere.

Day 24: It's A Living Thing

Ezekiel stands and stares at the gateway. He hears the sound of rushing water. Something is happening, something is coming at him. He flinches. Suddenly, the brightest light in the world smashes into his eyes. He ducks. Looks again, ducks down again. Looks up. Squints into the searing sunlight. The roaring sound grows louder, thundering and booming in his ears. It disorientates him. He has to drop to his knees before he falls over. He can't look at the light yet he can barely drag his eyes away. He uses his fingers as slats, intermittent protection from the shining up ahead. He knows now what it is. It can be nothing else. This is the glory of the God of Israel, this is what Moses saw, this is the energy and force that brought the planets into being, this is the invisible God showing his face a little. Peeking over the ledge of the world, putting in an appearance from the east. Sneaking a view of the world. The sound of his coming is like the roar of a million waterfalls, and the whole landscape shines with his glory as if it's burning up without being consumed. Ezekiel fears he will not make it through this, that it'll be a tale untold, a story that dies with him, right here, right now. But he recalls something. The Kebar River. He saw the glory like this that day, and he is still here to glimpse it again. He saw God and lived. Saw God and went home and entered the most baffling period of his life. Trapped indoors. Gagged, bound, no voice, no platform, no means to communicate what he'd seen. A glimpse of God but no permission to share it. Perhaps this time it will be different. Perhaps this time he will tell the world about the living God who shines like the sunrise and the sunset merged a thousand times over. No wonder Moses's face shone. This heat, this burning, this bright presence would leave anyone marked. His knees buckle and he bends forward, falls on his face, and nurses the ground with his hands. And he hears the movement, the glory passing by, the thunder swelling then receding, the light dimming to a distant glow and a few long shadows. He looks up, the last shards of light creep away. He breathes a sigh. He has seen the glory of God and lived. The glory of the Lord coming through that gateway. All the way from the east.

Jesus traipses in circles. His feet are dull and heavy. His lips move silently as he prays. There is no glory for him today. Just more waiting, more longing, more hunger. Inside he trusts that he is becoming something. Something that will bring Ezekiel's glory to the people in the street. But it won't look much like glory. It won't make the sound of glory, and it won't have the bright light. It'll just look like an ex-carpenter, holding out his scarred hand in front of a crowd to a small boy with a basket of rolls. It'll look like a travelling man stopping by to eat and drink at the wrong parties. It'll look like a criminal, bloody and cowering, waiting to die the same way so many other would-be Messiahs have done. It will look like nothing much at all. But it will be the glory of God. And it will come out of this desert.

- - - - - - - - - - -

'You mentioned the C word the other day.'
I sat back. It was late and the whisky was flowing, but even so, I wasn't expecting this from Brother B.
'The C word?'
'Commi-t-ment.'
He says it slowly, like Rowan Atkinson might, with the emphasis on the middle 't'.
I think. My turn for a story.
'Years ago, I mean years ago, decades. I fell for a Dutch girl. We met on holiday and then had to go our separate ways. As you can imagine much of the relationship was then conducted over the phone. I was sharing a house with a couple of mates and they had some of their friends over for a big splash of a party one night. I'd been on the phone to my girlfriend and felt very in love, as you do. I felt so in love that I went into the kitchen, which I hasten to add was piled high with dirty dishes, and I washed up every single plate, pan and knife they'd used. The lot. I felt so good that it was a pleasure to wash up for them. Love can do that eh?'
Brother Basil said nothing. I went on.
'Not long after that I ended the relationship. I lost the feelings and I panicked. The emotion drained away and I couldn't get back to that

night when I washed up those dishes. I didn't feel that way anymore. I was scared. Genuinely. I didn't understand what had happened, how I could feel so much one day, and lose it another. How could I love this girl if I felt nothing? And that's why commitment scared me. I couldn't understand it.'

'And later? With your wife?'

'I was lucky,' I said, 'other people cornered me, told me I was onto a good thing, bypassed my emotions if you like. I don't mean they ordered me to be in love with her, they just shored me up. Made me trust in something more. Something other, something that occupied a different place. Something objective I suppose.'

'Do you feel that was misguided now?' Brother Basil asks, caution in his voice. 'Their encouragement to trust?'

I shrug. I don't know. I don't think so.

'We had some good times. They couldn't have known it would unravel the way it did.' We sit in silence for a while and then I feel the need to fill it. 'Commitment is still a big thing for me,' I say.

'The problem with some of the best things in life is that they look all wrong. They don't look like the best things at all. Do you know what I mean?'

I don't but I give a half-nod to be polite.

'Well let me tease that out. Humility can make you look weak, like a doormat. Kindness can appear naïve. Hope can be seen as foolishness. Patience will get you labelled as boring. And concern for others will turn you into a do-gooder. Do you see what I mean? Jesus pointed this out, when he said that the world does it one way but God does it another. The way of the world is to do with looking right, impressing others, being seen to be seen. The way of Jesus is to do with impressing God. And commitment is one of those things, one of God's priorities. Most people don't realise it but when they get married they are sending a message to the world. A message that God loves – that sticking with someone is good. Now I don't mean sticking with someone who beats you every night and hurts your children and destroys your world. What I mean is this, marriage is a parable. When marriage works and there is give and take, and humility and kindness, then it is a story about the kind of commitment God offers us. It's not fashionable and many people don't believe in it anymore. And I am well aware that I am a single person saying this. But all I know is this. Two thousand years ago Jesus turned the way of the world on its head. He continues to do that today.'

As I stroll home to my shed, doing my best not to tumble due to the dark and the whisky, I recall a scene from the movie *Keeping The Faith*. Two priests sit there discussing love and commitment in a scene not unlike the one Brother Basil and I have just played out. The older one tells the younger that loving a woman is like being a priest, 'You cannot make a real commitment unless you accept that it's a choice that you keep making again and again and again.' He also adds that he's been a catholic priest for over forty years, and he fell in love at least once every decade…

Day 25: Turning Tables

So little happening. He should be out there changing things. The time is short. He should be doing something. He sits on a rock. Thinks briefly of bread. Again. Then other visions fill his head. A dead girl on a bed. Mourners laughing, a father with his face creased in despair and confusion. Then two sisters about to lose everything because their brother is in a tomb. They cannot inherit from him, they will lose the home they love, prostitution beckons. Then he sees people running, a garden at night, torches, swearing, men with fists for hands and curses for conversation. He shivers. A brighter scene, a man hurls seeds across a patch of land. Good soil, bad soil. Two men build a house nearby, one half of it is on rock, the other on boggy marshland. He wants to call out, warn them about that. Over in the other side of his mind some tenants take over a farm. They call it their own, refuse to recognise the legal owner. Notice is sent, there is violence. People die. Then another face, Archelaus, the man who was king when he was born. Very much the son of his father. Perpetuating the same greed and corruption. A crowd in the street hate him. Beg for a replacement. Anything is better than this. The king leaves, the people do not make the most of it. They dig holes and bury treasure instead. Another man finds treasure. Digs it up then buries it again. Goes looking to see who owns the field. Trades in everything he has so he can make a deal and get the treasure. Then he sees an angel walking the earth, collecting pearls on behalf of another kingdom. The visions fade. He stands, walks, talks to the sky. He knows his father is listening he just cannot see it or prove it. He walks on, smacks his toe against a rock and sits down to nurse it. If that rock had been bread this wouldn't have happened.

- - - - - - - - - - -

Mitch Levine is in a bad place. His hopes are smashed, his heart broken, his dreams lie in pieces like the fragments of last night's beer bottles swept in a heap on the pub steps. It's the end, he yells, the end, the end. A bitter and most melodic end. Till tomorrow, when his hopes will be dashed all over again and there'll be another end to sing about. I stand there, tapping my feet, nodding my head and listening in on Mitch's angst. Poor guy. The rich and famous have hard lives. Still, it makes me smile and fits my mood right now. The Giggheads can make any catastrophe sound like a good time. That's the snag with art. It does its best to mirror life but is always somehow that much more eloquent, that much more glamorous. In a movie if some guy is depressed then Amy Winehouse will be singing a complementary song about it in the background. In life you're just downright miserable. Reality doesn't come with a readymade soundtrack. And I guess Jesus didn't have an mp3 player to pipe in the songs from Lamentations just when he needed them. 'Oh God where are you? I feel like I've been attacked by a bear, beaten up and left for dead. My teeth ground in the dust and my face ripped and splintered by the sharp stones on my path.' Those guys could write a sad song all right. No idea if they had tunes like The Giggheads but either way, Jesus wouldn't have been able to tap his feet, nod his head and hum along in his wilderness. It just didn't work like that. I doubt that Adele's *Turning Tables* was playing as Jesus walked away from trashing the temple, his head hanging and heart breaking at the injustice of a system that hurts so many people. He was on his own, no Mitch Levine or Phat Phingers Franklin to cross his path. Ah, Phat Phingers Franklin. If only he was he… wait a minute… is… is that him? No. Can't be. Just imagining it. Getting carried away with the music. Aye, aye, it's lunch time. I saunter down still jigging a little too visibly to Mitch's music.

Phat Phingers is here! I'm sure of it. I'm sitting in the refectory eating my parsnip soup and I catch sight of a familiar face. Just opposite and three seats down. He's not good looking like Mitch and doesn't have the same presence but he's clearly in a rock band. The painted nails, black eyeliner and designer stubble are a bit of a giveaway. But it's the guitar slung over the back of his chair that clinches it. It's got a huge Giggheads logo on the base. This guy is almost rock royalty, maybe not Will and Kate level, but certainly Fergie's daughters. Which come to think of it, would not be a bad name for a rock band. Like Shakespeare's Sister, or Byron's Second Cousin Twice Removed. I try not to stare at the lead guitarist from The Giggheads but it's too difficult. When else will I slurp mushy parsnips opposite the guy who wrote that feelgood classic *You're In My Tuna Sandwich*. He looks up, I glance away and then back. He's still looking. He nods faintly as if to say, 'Yea, you got it. Now let me eat my parsnip soup.' So I nod back and do just that. He's a little bit scary actually.

I don't stop and chat to him. Well, you know, things to do, people to see. And I'm disappointed again. I'm disappointed that I can be held to ransom by the close proximity of a pop star. Where was Brother Ben today? Is he okay? I have no idea because I was too busy ogling Phat Phingers. I wonder if I could get his autograph in my Bible? Why? Why do I want that? What's the point? I know, I'll get Brother Ben's autograph.

I sigh as I walk, ram the earplugs into the sides of my head and play the last track on *Long John Silver's Missing Leg*. It wasn't written by Phat Phingers. Or Mitch. This one is credited to the drummer. Johnnie Quango. I've not really given it a proper listen till now. Turns out it's a story song. Starts off sounding like *We Will Rock You* but pretty soon turns into something more like Bruce Springsteen's *Jungleland*. Man, this drummer can write. I love it. It's a kind of parable. Called *Meeting Me*. A guy down on his luck finds himself in a strange town, wanders into a bar called *The See You Round*. Turns out be a place full of himself at different ages in his life. He spends the rest of the song drinking beer with the various incarnations of himself at ages ten, fifteen, twenty and thirty bantering about the mistakes he made and getting advice from the earlier prototypes. The final heartbreaking verse features his seventy year-old self, projected into the future, giving some coded warnings about the futility of harbouring bitterness, loving his work too much, and staring at the green grass on the other side of the fence. As the guitars play out I'm left with a vision of the guy getting up, walking out into the night having found himself, and being somewhat disappointed and frustrated by the experience. Somehow The Giggheads still make this wistful number sound like a celebration though. The saddest songs turn into a carnival in their hands. It's their rare talent I think, taking the hard things in life, holding back on the sheen, and putting them out there in all their complex glory. Tough tunes that stick in your head and won't go away. The guy in Johnnie Quango's tale is never named. So you can imagine the seven minutes of that stuff and you feel you're the poor stranger who's been to *The See You Round* and back again.

He even meets a celebrity version of himself. Famous, successful and sad. Having got it all, it's somehow still not what he wanted. It's a well-known truth. But the song brings it home again. The tune might help me not forget it.

Brother Ben appears from nowhere. Towering above me as he does. Grinning, waving a TUC biscuit in my general direction.
   'Still The Giggheads?' he asks as I pull the plugs out.
I nod.
   'Let me guess… *Meeting Me*? *The See You Round*?'
How did he know that?
He taps his temple, then says, 'Intuition… plus I caught you mouthing the words there. Weird idea eh?'
   'I loved it.'
   'Man it would freak me, suppose you'd got everything wrong? Suppose all those other versions of yourself just had a go at you?'
I think about that. 'I'm an optimist,' I lie and he laughs.
   'You just like a good story, mate,' he says, 'plus the tune's a killer.'
He starts to walk back to the kitchen then stops, turns back.
   'Wanna come on a night-walk with me? Kind of like a meditation thing? Me and Fin are going tonight at midnight.'
   'Okay,' I say before I can really ponder the option and reconsider it.
   'Cool!' he says, looking genuinely pleased. '11.45 down in the refectory, I'll make sure the door's left open. Got a torch? No worries, I'll get one. Wrap up warm, and bring waterproofs and maybe something to drink. No, don't worry, I'll bring a flask of tea. Got any Bourbons left? Excellent. You bring the bread I'll bring the wine.'

I head back for my shed with a certain spring in my step. Not really such a good idea 'cause I smack the side of my foot straight into a rock and it hurts. It really hurts. Johnnie's song was sad but it made me feel much better than stubbing my ankle. I try and conceal it but it's no good, I hop and hobble the rest of the way.

Day 26: In The Midnight Hour

'There are times when the most miraculous things in the world come disguised as the most mundane, when what is precious turns up wearing clothes pinched from a rubbish tip. Beware. Things may seem unimportant when they are valuable indeed.'
Up The Creek Having Burnt The Paddle by Pew Hadovood

- - - - - - - - - - -

It's dark and cold. And for the first time I wonder about the nights in the Judean wilderness. Did Jesus take some skins, a blanket? His cousin John had been out in the wilderness, had he prepared him? Did they talk about what he might need for his extreme retreat. We meet at 11.50pm, I'm a little late but then so is Brother Ben. Brother Fin is bang on time. He seems a gentle, quiet guy. Short, mid-thirties, cropped ginger hair, looks a little like a small version of Chris Evans. Not that I know how tall Mr Evans is, but Fin appears shorter. Suddenly get a daft idea and pull out my Bible, not quite sure why I brought it for a night ramble but I did. I ask him if he'll autograph it for me. He looks a little bewildered. Those ginger eyebrows bump into each other then bounce apart like a couple of repelling magnets. He takes the Bible and slips it open. I don't have a pen. Neither does he. I obviously didn't come prepared for a celebrity moment. Neither of us did. He holds up a hand and disappears. Brother Ben turns up.
   'Got the biscuits?' he asks, super-spiritual as ever.
I smile and nod. I pat my rucksack, there's a jumper in there too. He takes the bag and turns it in his hands.
   'Nice,' he says, tapping his finger on the ancient *Clash* graphic.
I look embarrassed. 'You could add The Giggheads to that now,' he says quickly and hands it back.
For some reason that doesn't seem such a bad idea. I'll definitely get Brother Ben's autograph. Brother Fin comes back in with a pen. He signs with a flourish and hands the Bible back to me.
   'What's that?' asks Ben.
Second moment of embarrassment in an inordinately short time.

'Will you sign it for me?' I say, 'I'm autograph hunting.'

Ben's face lights up. 'Really? You sure? Okay.'

His is much more of a scrawl. He's in the process of handing it back then stops, the book hovering between us.

'Hey, you know who's here don't you?

Of course I do, but I just shrug.

'Phat Phingers! You should get his autograph.'

I adopt the kind of look that sort of says, 'Not thought of that. I'll mull it over. Thanks for the advice.'

'I'm telling you, if you want an autograph, there's a star for you. I mean, come on, he did write *You're In My Tuna Sandwich* you know.'

'What's he doing here? Did Mitch tell him to come?'

Brothers Ben and Fin laugh. I join in though I don't really know why I'm laughing. Just trying to be one of the gang I suppose.

Ben shakes his head. 'Doubt it, this was hell on earth for Mitch. He couldn't see the point of peace and quiet. No, I think Phat probably heard about it from him, but he's here under his own steam. He's a more ambient kind of guy. He likes a bit of cow dung and country. My theory is they're thinking about splitting up.'

But they've only just got going!

'In your life maybe, but The Giggheads have been together for ten years. That's a lot of rock'n'roll parties, a lot of unsuccessful singles, and a big cult following. I think Mitch wants to be Mr Solo. Anyway come on. The night's young, we gotta walk.'

We strike out and that's when the cold really bites, it's not long before I'm digging into my rucksack for that spare jumper. We walk in silence, the ground crunching and scraping beneath our boots. Brother Fin says very little, Ben chatters here and there, aiming his conversation at no one in particular. After an hour he breaks out the tea and I get the Bourbons.

'When do we do the spiritual stuff?' I ask.

They glance at each other. 'What do you mean?'

'You know, the meditation bit?'

'This is it, mate, doesn't get more spiritual than this. The night, the stars, the quiet, the dark. God's all around. Just get into a rhythm with your walking and absorb the happening of it all. Not even The Giggheads could make this better.'

'Really? You mean we won't be stopping to do Bible readings?'
Ben laughs, a great belly laugh.

'No. Nothing against that, nothing at all. But we came out here to get away from all that. This is God in the dark. No prescription, no study notes, no sermons. Other than the night. Kind of what Jesus had in his wilderness boot camp, eh? Don't think he took any Hebrew scriptures with him. Didn't have a first century e-reader with any Dead Sea Scrolls on it... what would you call that? An iParchment I guess!'
Ben and Fin both laugh at this.

'No seriously bro, we're just doing the best thing. Walking in the dark. Praying by being here. Cuts out any of those words we might feel we're supposed to say in front of God.'

'Silence is sometimes the best form of honesty,' Brother Fin suddenly puts in, which startles me, as he's said next to nothing since the autograph incident.

So we drink tea, chew biscuits and walk again. And the night gets closer, and our eyes grow accustomed, and there is noise everywhere. The quiet fills with sound. Footsteps, creatures, rustling, breathing. But no cars or pubs turning out or lads trying to outdo each other. Not even in their praying. And somewhere in it all, I tell myself, there is the voice of God. Though he may not be saying anything too profound. Just walking with us, without feeling the need to keep talking out loud.

Day 27: The Walk Of Life

He stands there and stares. Another vision. The temple rises in front of him, like shimmering heat on the noon horizon. And that gate again, the one in the east wall. But it's locked. No. More than that. Bricked up. Colossal stones stand in the gap. No one can go through now. Why? What's happened here? What's going on? Somewhere in his mind or deep in his soul he hears the voice of his father. 'This gate must remain closed now; it will never again be opened. The glory of God has been through it. No man will pass through, for the Lord, the God of Israel, entered here. Look, your king comes, riding on a donkey…' The images merge again in his mind. The crowds, the east gate, the donkey, the soldiers. The temple begins to shake like a child with fever, then the walls become a parchment of cracks and fissures, bits of stone break off and tumble down, there is a thunderous noise. The shouts of war and the screams of the innocent. Pounding feet, running for the hills. Pounding feet, invading the temple. There is fire and murder. The place lies in ruins. Silence. The desert is silent. The vision is silent. Nothing now, just wasteland. The walls have fallen. The temple is dying. His heart breaks as he watches, then that distant voice again. 'Take a look, I make all things new.' And another vision, a new building, a temple full of light, a city pouring living water across the desert. The floodgates open and the water pours towards him, as it slides across the desert the ground wakes again, things begin to grow, plants, vegetation, trees. The tallest trees. Birds fly in, make nests, shelter in the branches. All kinds of life appear. Animals, crops, trees that shouldn't grow in this place. Nothing stops them, the temple pours the living water and the land drinks deeply. And the people come, flooding like the water, the young the old, rich and poor, all shapes and sizes, from every nation and land. He sits down exhausted. Shuts his eyes. Waits for the world to come to rest. He opens his eyes again. He is alone. The desert is back. The wilderness. The rocks. The quiet and the familiar. But he has glimpsed something, he has seen where all this is heading.

- - - - - - - - - - -

I learnt something last night. I just don't know what it was. Tramping through the dark with two guys I barely know, no idea where we were headed, I felt this kind of weight lift. No responsibility. Could have ended in disaster. They could have been out to abduct me. Or we could have been savaged by wolves. Or I might have slipped into a ditch and broken a leg. Any number of disastrous things. I can't explain it but I just felt free. Like it could have all ended out there on the moor and it would have been all right. Reflecting now as I lie in bed I realise how rare that feeling is, that I spend most of my life uptight. Not in any way abandoned or relaxed. Not letting life just come to me because I have to be on my guard. Anything could happen and I rarely see that as a good thing. The unexpected is bad. It's not a broad open space where anything is possible, it's a jungle full of killers. Walking in the dark made me see that and for a short time I changed. I saw another world, other possibilities.

Control is such a restrictive thing. I define myself by my tenuous hold on life. Making sure it's all in place. My faith, my work, my routines, my relationships. Last night I lost all that. I didn't even have tabs on God. He could have been anywhere. Why does life narrow me down? Why does it not lead me into a bigger place? A place where things are possible. An open space where a little water can make the unexpected live.

I reach for my Bible and flip it open. The first thing I see is the two autographs. Not Mitch and Phat Phingers but Ben and Fin. I flick pages until I find Ezekiel. My favourite book. I love this guy, the biblical Robin Williams. Cooks, mimes, cuts hair, makes models, plays with dung, demolishes walls, poses, acts, falls down and gets up again – all in the name of prophecy. He'll do anything to get the message to the people. Words are not enough for this maverick; actions speak louder. Stories too, he tells a gripping yarn. His pages are strewn with adventures that wouldn't look out of place in Smiths and Waterstones - *The Storm Cloud and the Four Faces, The Scorpion's Sting, Bound and Gagged, The Model Siege, Ready Steady Cow Dung, The Skinhead, The Unlovely Bones, Money for Trash, The Sun Worshippers, Six Killers and a Writer, The Glowing Coals*. He's most famous for his trip to the valley of death. Random bones of the long dead reform into skeletons and morph back into a living army in a scene that looks like something from *The Mummy Returns*. But I flip another ten chapters from there. To a long and arguably tedious account of his vision of the temple. Water pours from the place, it takes a long time, getting deeper and deeper and deeper as it revives the land. This is no ordinary water, this is living water, the kind of stuff Jesus said would pour from human beings. God's remedy for a dying world, new life coming out of those who have started to live again. In Ezekiel's day the temple was the perfect place for this to start. But later Jesus would adjust the picture. Refocus the lens. Temples are no longing building-shaped. Now they look like people. Now the water gushes from heroes like Ben and Fin. Reviving losers like me.

I know that's what I sensed last night. Like skinny dipping in the waters of life. Shocking and liberating. That's probably what Jesus had in mind when he came up with the deal about offering us the truth so it would set us free. Not so that we could package it neatly and carry it around in our back pockets, or fax it to others who wanted an identical copy. If the truth sets me free, and if I dare take up the offer of swimming in the water of life, then you can sure as hell bet the outcome for me won't look the same as the outcome for you. Freedom sets us free. I tasted that last night, and Ben and Fin had the grace to let it happen.

Day 28: It's The End Of The World As We Know It

He could play it safe. It would be easier, save him a lot of trouble. He could sidestep the temple issue altogether. Upset no one. Resurrection might be a problem. Reviving people is inevitable. There are so many lifeless around. He's bound to resurrect their hopes, dreams, bodies, purpose, faith. It's unavoidable and the issue will annoy the Sadducees like mad. They will hate it. All it needs is a couple of corpses back on their feet acting like death was just a stubbed toe and the temple aristocrats will go through the roof. It's against their religion. People just don't come back to life, not in their worldview. So that's bound to be trouble and can't be avoided. But the temple… that's another story. With a little sidestepping and some carefully chosen words he can dodge criticising the corruption and money making. He can see that this might save his life. Conflict with the Pharisees is inevitable, not because they're all bad, far from it. He's spent many a happy hour bantering with those self-appointed policemen of the faith. He knows they mean well, they want the nation back on its feet and the best way to do that is to keep the law. That will bring God back to his people. Or so they think. The truth is God has been with his people for a while now, they just didn't know it. But they will soon. The dead will live and the word will spread. The gutters will run with forgiveness and justice and it will be clear that something is up.

There will be conflict but the Pharisees are not dangerous like the Sadducees. It won't be the Pharisees that get murderously upset about his challenge to the temple and its taxes. It will be the money men. Caiaphas and his father-in-law. He arranges a few rocks in a temple shape on the ground. Adds details to flesh out the picture. This home of God. This ancient building, the centre of all that is Jewish. Faith, life, future. It's all in the temple. So who is he to come along and start talking about a new kind of temple? One made of people, flesh and blood. With himself as the foundation rock. If he says too much about this it won't be long before word gets back to the corridors of power in Jerusalem. Just don't start talking about knocking it down, he tells himself as he adds the finishing touches to his street picture. That would be sedition. That would get him a place on a death list. He sweeps his hand across the ground. The temple tumbles as the rocks go spinning. He sighs. It's inevitable. Regrettable but inevitable. The system is just too corrupt.

- - - - - - - - - - -

Deserts are not necessarily physical places. I'm learning that. You often don't need to go anywhere different at all. The world around you, the familiar, the friendly, the ordered, it starts to change. The solid ground suddenly feels more like sinking sand. The air becomes dry and dust-clogged, making it hard to breathe. And the temperature starts to rise. The sky fills with blistering sun and the heat is unbearable. Things that were once familiar landmarks change shape, becoming mere apparitions. And peace and purpose are nothing more than cruel mirages. All of that can come about in a single day. Less, a single hour. Or the briefest of moments.

'I lost my job Ben.'

He nods a big nod, one that uses his head and shoulders. Something he often does when he's listening to me.

'That's tough,' he says.

'Do monks ever get fired?'

He thinks. 'Doubt it. They run away. And I suppose they can get thrown out for bad behaviour, you know, breaking the vows. But it's not like being fired.'

'Did you ever lose a job?'

He nods. 'Paper round,' he says. 'Another kid was faster, and a better aim with his papers. Plus he didn't turn up half an hour late from time to time. Do you have a plan?'

He offers me a Polo.

'Not yet. Hope to concoct something while I'm here.'

'What do you mean? God will drop something out of the sky?'

'No. I just need to get my head straight, shake off some of the bad things that have dogged me lately. Can hardly think straight some days. Things have happened pretty fast. Six months ago I was married with a job and a baby on the way. Now I live in a shed.'

'Yea – but it is "The Shack", you never know what'll happen.'

'Brother Wilf, he's the oldest guy here, he's about a hundred and seven I think, he says look at the clues. What do you do already? What are you good at? What makes you angry and passionate?'

I think. I don't know. Not anymore. It's not that I don't have the information, I just can't access it with my mind full of the last six months. My retrieval system is on hold.

'I like movies,' I say, suddenly grabbing at straws.

'There you go – easy – work in a cinema.'

I give him my best 'Pursue this line and I might punch your lights out' look.

'What?' He holds up his hands.

'I worked in a cinema before. Remember? It was a nightmare. I told you. Good things came out of it, I became much more honest and realistic about life and faith, but I don't want to go back there. I don't want to become any more honest and realistic thanks. I'm done with honesty and realism now.'

I'm a little disappointed he doesn't recall our heart-to-heart about this, but why should he? It was my car-wreck of a job, not his.

'I'll talk to Brother Fin – he's a quiet guy but his brain is like a swamp, it's full of stuff. Good stuff. I'll ask him.'

Brother Fin. Makes appalling pea soup and I have his autograph. He's pretty good at kicking a football and now he's going to plan my future.

Ah well, someone has to.

Day 29: One Of Us

'Time moves slowly. We may urge it on, do our best to speed it up, occupy our days so that we don't notice its gentle passing. But ultimately time is a slow-moving vehicle. It does not hurry or race against itself. It merely moves on, perpetual motion. Watching it move is like watching paint dry, or dust settle. Not much happens. Time is a difficult gift, one that will not have meaning in heaven. Imagining that sort of thing in this life is impossible, like thinking up a new colour, or getting inside someone else's skin. The best thing we can do with time is mix it with the good things in life.'
Up The Creek Having Burnt The Paddle by Pew Hadovood

- - - - - - - - - - -

I break bread as usual, and as often happens there is a knock at the door as I pour the tea. It is a stranger. An older chap, white beard, baseball cap, earring, little round glasses. Ben Gunn pops into my mind for some reason. He holds out a weathered hand. The nails are blackened and splintered, the fingers red and cracked.

'Doug,' he says. 'A little bird told me you do a strange kind of communion here.'
Now I'm not good with just inviting strangers into my life, and right now my shed is my life. So I keep him on the doorstep. He scratches at his beard.

'I don't have to come in,' he says.
Good. It's a bright day, spring's doing its best again, I bring the tea out. I roll up a tree stump for Doug and sit on a mound of earth.

'They say you've been here a while,' he says.
I nod. It's four weeks now. Four weeks! Can it really be that long since I threw my bag on that bed and contemplated life with an outside toilet?

'So,' he waves his Bourbon at me, 'bread and wine eh?'
He has a habit of winking with his right eye at the end of each sentence.

'I'm what you might call low church,' I say. 'Tea and biscuits, coffee and doughnuts, Coke and crisps.'

'Bread and dripping,' Doug chuckles.

'To me it's about food reminding me of God.'

'What sort of a God?'

'What?'

'What sort of a God is tea and biscuits?'

'Well... you know. Jesus.'

'Oh Jesus.'

We sit and slurp tea. Doug dunks his biscuit, barely makes it to his mouth before it breaks off, then grabs another from the packet.

'What about Jesus?' he says.

'Where do you want me to start? He's God... in jeans and a jacket. God up close. God who understands what it means to you and me to sit outside sharing tea and biscuits. God who knows our stories and doesn't judge.'

'Doesn't judge?'

'No, he specifically said that. 'I haven't come to judge the world, but to rescue it.' That sort of thing.'

Doug thinks about this for a while, scratches his beard then plays with his earring.

'I done some things,' he said. 'Feels like I did get judged. Made mistakes. That's all, made mistakes. But the judgement was heavy. Can't get that out of my head. Feels like he's watching me all the time.'

'Did you ever have one of those kind of "God is watching you" quotes on the wall,' I ask in a moment of inspiration.

'Christ is the unseen guest,' says Doug with a sad shake of the head.

'Can I tell you a secret?' I say and Doug leans in a little.

'I went to a grammar school right? And it was in the days when we referred to each other by our surnames. And you know what now? I don't like calling Jesus 'Christ' – it sounds like his surname and I'd rather call him by his first name. Christ seems too distant, too hard, like I don't know him very well.'

'Meaning what?'

'Meaning... Christ may be the unseen guest but Jesus ain't. Jesus is the man who invited himself round to eat with Zacchaeus who, if you don't mind me saying, was a bit like you. Jesus went round his house. Actually, I've just realised that's the wrong way round. You're like Jesus and it's me that's like Zacchaeus. 'Cause you've invited yourself round and here we are chewing on life and forgiveness. So there you go.'

Doug says nothing.

'He didn't judge Zacchaeus, Doug,' I say and he looks up when I mention his name. 'You may well spend the rest of your days feeling like the unseen guest is judging you, but Jesus never does. It's not why he came.'

Doug nods and he gets up and wanders off leaving me wondering if I crossed a line somewhere. I stay sitting on the mound of earth for a long time but he doesn't come back. The waiting makes me aware that I can do this. Sit around with no agenda other than waiting for Doug, a visitor I didn't want, yet who in some strange way turned into Jesus for me. I think about the judgement I fear from the unseen guest. Dead easy to tell someone else to not fear it. Dead easy. I sit there for a long time.

Day 30: Pride (In the Name of Love)

He needn't have come up here. He's placed himself in the firing line by doing this. But it's time, he senses it. So he stands on the high place and looks. The dark figure approaches. Moving nearer up the side of the mount. No greeting. Just straight in. The figure holds out his hand and snap! A thousand kingdoms appear. Leaders arise. The wealth of the world is right there in his palm. Control. Government. Authority. It's all waiting for him. It's his. He simply has to change his focus, adjust his vision. Look in the wrong direction. Worship the wrong thing. He raises his other palm and sees the future in it. Sees all those other things people may choose to worship. Benign things gone bad. Religious symbols become gods. The channels to God becoming the face of God. Buildings, traditions, language. People will argue, fight, kill each other over these. Worship will become war. Dedication will turn to death. God is love, but the wrong worship will make him look like hate. This is a deep-seated issue. This invitation to worship. Bow down and you can have what you want. That's what it comes down to, well, he hasn't come into the wilderness to get what he wants. He's come to get something else. He's come to get into shape, the right shape to bring a new age. And you can't carry a new age in your hand if you're carrying all the power on earth in there too. There is not enough room for both. He will leave the quest for earthly power and take up something else. He will take up the way of peace, and he knows millions of others will do the same. He sees their faces now, so many people no one else will ever see. No plaudits or accolades or medals for these. Millions of unknowns without the power to rule, exercising their power to care. He stands, he turns. He hears his own words as they spill from his mouth. 'Fear the Lord your God and serve only him.' He walks away.

- - - - - - - - - -

The toilet hasn't been cleaned. Not since I arrived. Four weeks of me and whoever else has been availing themselves of my facilities is enough. I decide to bite the bullet. Brother Ben gets me a bucket and some disinfectant. I'm on my knees on the hard concrete floor, wondering what so many of the stains are. Not sure if Jesus ever cleaned a toilet but he cleaned feet that had practically walked through one. He never said, 'Blessed are those who get their hands dirty,' but he might as well have. Certainly getting my hands dirty now. I mean – there's dirt and there's dirt. Mud and grit are one thing. But the remnants of a million lavatory users are something else entirely. This place may well have not been cleaned since it was used by Guy Fawkes. It's certainly seen some action. Hunched there on my knees, my nose too close to pungent matter, I start thinking about feet. Not mine necessarily, other people's. Jesus broke bread, poured wine and washed feet. Then he said, 'Do this and remember me.' Can't help thinking we may have forgotten to do a certain part of that little ritual. Bread and wine, great, fantastic. Feet? Er… I'll get my coat.

I hear a footstep behind me, look round. White beard, baseball cap. It's Doug.

'Just wanted a tinkle,' he says.

I stand up, dust my hands.

'Be my guest I say,' stepping back and deciding enough is enough.

He taps his cap and shuffles in. As I wait I can't help looking around, there are dozens of bushes nearby. Wouldn't one of those have been okay for Doug right now? Well… it's not good enough for me, so not for him I guess. He's not in there long. There is no sound of flushing so I go in and do it for him. He nods.

'Tea?' he asks.

Tea. I make it. We sit outside again, him on the stump, me on the bank.

'I thought about what you said,' he says. 'Seems all too easy, like you can get away with anything. I mean God is God, right? He ain't some two bit street kid hanging around on the corner waiting for a bus.'

'I agree. But we're small, our minds cannot hold the full picture. I agree that the Old Testament picture of God sometimes give us the *thunder and lightning on the smoky mountain* kind of image of God, but the glory of God in the New Testament is powerful in a different way. There's no doubt that God is awesome, and I don't mean in the teenage "he's so cool" kind of way. But if Jesus is about anything, he's about a God who has made himself smaller, accessible, approachable, understanding. He washes feet and sits down with the poor. He gives us room to manoeuvre.'

'Does he?' Doug says. 'But the church says you got to behave properly and dress up right and give lots of money.'

Silence. I try and think of a useful question.

'Were you a member of a church once?' I ask him.

'Of course. But they threw me out.'

'I'm sorry.'

'Yea, me too. Well... I was and I wasn't. I couldn't really fit in and I didn't see why so many things seemed important. I went 'cause I needed help but everyone else seemed worried about other stuff. There was a big argument about what hymns we sang and whether to buy a new carpet. They were raising money for it when there were folks like me who had no job.' A pause, then, 'D'you like God?'

'Do I like him?'

'Yea, well so many people fight and argue about him, and even kill each other! It's crazy. Religion just seems to make people angry.'

'Well I think we all get our own ideas about what's important, we can't always see God very clearly. Like trying to picture someone through a dirty window – too many streaks and stains get in the way. But when you read about Jesus in the Bible he seems to go out of his way to meet people that feel rejected. People that don't fit in with our churches and organisations. People on the edge. The folks who won't look right or smell right.'

Doug thinks on this then says,

'Are you saying I don't smell right?'

Well, yes actually, but I shake my head. A little too quickly perhaps.

'Of course not.'

He grins.

'I know what you're saying,' he says. 'I get it.'

I shut up. We sit there and munch on biscuits. I'm preaching to myself really.

Day 31: Wondrous Stories

Stories are good. He has plenty now, a real armoury of ideas and folk tales gleaned from the desert, from the past, from home and from his huge fertile imagination. He will revisit history, draw on the lives of his listeners, shock and entertain. Hurl out pearls wrapped up in parables, wisdom launched out there like a fistful of seed. And he will watch carefully, see who is listening, who is hungry, who wants to debate and chew on them. Who can see themselves in the tall tales. They will be like little pictures, cartoons, exaggerations on life, images once heard never forgotten. Thieves, bandits, widows, treasure, fools, heroes... the characters race through his mind, like children chasing one another down the street. He stares at the dust, the list of stories he has made in it with his finger. A movement to one side, he flicks his eyes, a scorpion. Black tail flexed in the air. Basking on a rock. Those rocks again, so bread-like. Scorpions and bread. Manna. God's gift. From nowhere a question creeps into his mind. If someone asks you for food, say an egg, would you hand out a scorpion? Would you give rocks to your children and call it bread? No. Of course not. People are rebellious and hot-headed and yet can do plenty of good things. And when they do good things, they are imitating God. He smiles. Another little story for his collection. The scorpion goes. Its job done. The rock remains, doing a wonderful impression of a hunk of fresh bread.

- - - - - - - - - - -

The Giggheads are singing about *The End Of The World In A Fast Food Drive Thru*. Someone has forgotten to reorder the cheese for the burgers. 'Gherkins would have been okay,' Mitch sings, 'Gherkins would have been fine. But not the golden slivers of cheese. Without the cheese it feels like the end of time.' The traffic's backing up and the guy in the kiosk can't cope with the irate customers and their quarter pound of rage. Fights break out, anarchy spreads, riots kick in and before you know it we're at war with China. 'Nuclear buttons are bared, trigger fingers play with the gun, all because the wafers of cheese went tragically AWOL under the bun.'

I have a headache. Being here is not making me feel better right now. My sleeping pattern is wrecked, my diet strange and macabre. I've failed at fasting, my prayer life is shot to pieces. I channel-hop books of the Bible, and haven't made much headway into any of the classics on my e-reader. In spite of the glowing recommendations. (*'A book for our time.' 'Everyone should read this before their days are up.' 'Funnier than the world's funniest joke.'*) Instead I spend most of my time listening to a feelgood band who sing sad songs about cheese. I'm not becoming the Ghandi-man I hoped I would. Looks like I won't be heading out to convert Milton Keynes or Bognor Regis or Little Piddlethwaite any time soon. The wilderness has not turned out to be the well-ordered, disciplined, tidy place I expected it to be. Right now it doesn't even feel spiritual.

I go looking for Brother Ben.
    'Did The Giggheads write any songs about God?' I ask him when I find him quietly reading his Bible on a bench in the quad. His version of the good book looks like a well-thumbed airport paperback. I half expect the cover to sport a blonde with a gun and a glass of champagne.
    'Songs about God?' he rubs his chin and sucks on his bottom lip like a wise old mountain man.
    'They did a great version of Andy Williams's *It's my happy heart you hear.*'
    'And is that about God?'
    'Nnnn...o. But it makes you feel as if it is. It's just so good. As is God.'
What?
    'Well look, songs don't have to say the name of God to be about him do they? And actually, Brother Baz told me that some songs which claim to be about God aren't really up to much at all. Take Jesus right?'
    'He didn't write songs.'
    'Nope, but his stories don't all have God in them.'
    'Don't they?'
    'Nope. Not at all. Good Samaritan – episode of *Casualty*. The farmer going out sowing seeds – *Emmerdale Farm*. The prodigal son – that

movie *The Beach* with Leonardo whatshisface. We know they're about God 'cause they're in here.'

He waves his airport paperback at me.

'But God isn't in the story, we just got used to looking for him there. See?'

And he goes back to reading.

'So, are there any Giggheads songs where you can find God?'

'Of course. You got twelve on your mp3 right there. Listen a bit harder, you might spot a few stories about him on there.'

Cheese? And the end of the world? I don't think so.

I earplug my ears and start to walk away.

'Take that track about fast food,' he suddenly calls again. 'Could be a parable about the danger of the wrong priorities.'

'But it's a funny story.'

'So is the one about the guy who has a tree trunk in his eye and yet tells his mate off for having a speck of sawdust on his eyelash. Trust me. Cheese and China. It's all about what really matters.'

I jump to the track about *The See You Round*. I'll chew on the cheese later.

Day 32: Everybody Hurts

'The desert is different. It's not so much a place where we encounter difficulty, but a place of difficulty. It is the nature of the desert to be hard, a place where our own problems find a home. Perhaps that's why Jesus regularly visited it, he had learnt that his troubles would be at home there. He could take his frustrations and fears and loneliness and pain and know he could lay them out on the desert floor. They fit in perfectly. They would not be at all out of place alongside rocks and scorpions and dry, dry dust.'
Up The Creek Having Burnt The Paddle by Pew Hadovood

- - - - - - - - - - -

I remember them both very clearly. Those two days. The day we found out we were going to have a baby. Then the day we found out we were not going to have a baby. Neither was anything like I imagined. The first day I had my mind on other things, was worried about the car and the coming holiday and getting everything fixed and sorted. Suddenly my head was in turmoil, shock, wonder, amazement, a too-good-to-be-true morning. Life stopped for a while. Because life had started inside my wife. Incredible.

The second day, two months later, I fell apart. Visibly. We both did. A stranger, and an angel disguised as a nurse perhaps, perched on the side of the hospital bed and said a few words I'll always remember. 'God is with you in this.'
And because she was a stranger, and because she didn't know us, and because she had the courage and compassion to do that, I knew it was true. God right there in that little desert in that hospital room. In that place of loss and pain and trouble. He wasn't a stranger to that experience. I was. I had never encountered that kind of thing before. I hadn't needed a stranger to tell me God was with us the day we discovered the baby. But I needed one the day we lost it.

My eyes are wet. Thank God I'm alone. Thank God. I lie on my mattress and stare at the shed ceiling, sniffing and breathing hard. There are all kinds of stains up there. Dead flies and spiders. Faded brown blotches. Cobwebs on the beams. It was presumably once clean and bright up there, like my life. But not now. Now it's murky and messy and dotted with the unexpected.

I sit up, sigh and reach for my Bible. That rough guide to desert living. Abraham's in a wilderness, crossing a desert, going nowhere. Called out into the unknown by God. Leaving behind his old life, leaving behind his days without an heir. Sarah has no children. The family will fade away. In Abraham's days you lived on through your kids. So they have a choice. Stay put and die or step into the wilderness and find new life. Take a risk and be fruitful. So they go. And it all goes wrong. Famine. No baby. No new life. What to do? Run of course. Run to something else. Egypt. Food. Provision. Distraction. Abraham has those stars every night to remind him that the impossible will happen. But even heroes have their Mr Bean moments. Moses was heading somewhere in his wilderness and yet never arrived. It all fell apart for him too. He was on the brink of going into his new life when the people bucked and pulled back. Moses died in his desert. Abraham too. But not Joseph and his designer coat. His brothers wanted him dead in the desert, so they threw him in a hole. But there were other plans. A long and winding road full of them. Elijah wanted to die in his wilderness. But angels had other plans for him, wouldn't let him starve to death. God was waiting in a cave. In the very place he ran to escape. He limped back. A different man. And so did Jesus. He came out too. It wasn't the desert that killed him.

Some people spend their whole lives in deserts. Pain, regret, depression, illness. It never leaves. They have to adjust. And all those things that I take for granted are not on offer to them. Florence Nightingale spent her last fifty years sick in bed. Apparently she did much of her world-changing propped up on pillows. Millions of people I'll never know wake up every day in slums and refugee camps. The notion of being upwardly mobile does not feature. They will wake up this way every day. They can't just choose to live in a shed for forty days. They are born in one.

Faith is a strange thing. We all have it, use it when we turn on the tap or start a new life with someone, found a charity or buy a bigger TV. We believe these things will make a difference, lead us somewhere new. Faith often takes imagination. The ability to see the world differently. What can I imagine right now? I won't always be in this shed. Soon my life will catch up with me again. Brother Ben and Brother Basil will be a memory. And then what? Where will my journey take me? Where will my faith put my feet then?

Tomorrow I am going to fast all day. It will sharpen me up, maybe help me see something new. Adjust my vision. Plus it will be a good discipline for me. I know my track record on food abstinence has been about as good as England's post-sixties attempts at world cup glory, but this will be different. A new day. This time I will do it. I feel so good about the idea that I want to start right now, but you can't start fasting when you've eaten so much you're full anyway.

Day 33: Help!

'When Jesus entered into the full experience of life it must have taken him into some inglorious places. After all, I need a God who has visited the dark corners of failure and frustration, as well as the high points of hope. I need a God who has spent time with my kind of mistakes in some way.'
Up The Creek Having Burnt The Paddle by Pew Hadovood

- - - - - - - - - - -

I feel sick.

I'm a complete failure at the fasting. It was a stupid idea. Lasted till 9.37am then binged on biscuits. A whole packet of Bourbons. And then all those Crawfords (now McVities) Cheddars I brought with me. Why can't I be like those men in the Christian paperbacks? Why can't I found global ship ministries and set up international Christian skiing holidays? How will I ever conquer the world for God if I can't rebuke a packet of cookies once in a while? I'm a failure. There's no other word for it. Failure failure failure. I hate myself.

I'm sitting here now staring at the empty wrapper, feeling like death is working its way through my veins, its fingers flexing for my throat, when there's a hefty knock at the door. It's Brother Ben.
    'Why so serious, dude?' he asks, making his way in and flopping on my mattress.
I feel an idiot, don't even manage to explain it well. But he gets it instantly.
    'Done it a million times bro. Who hasn't? You'll do better another day.'
But I was going to fast all day.
    'Been there, done that, got the chicken tikka,' he says. 'Seriously, you can't kill yourself over a few biscuits.'
Actually it's a few biscuits, four cups of tea, some old Polo mints and a hunk of bread from yesterday.

'Feel a bit sick actually.'

He laughs.

'Look at me!' I moan, 'I try to be a giant of the faith and end up looking like a spiritual hobbit.'

'Hobbits are good. Apart from the hairy feet and the lack of ability to play basketball. But they eat well. And their heart is good. Better to be a hobbit than a ring wraith eh?'

We've gone a little too far into the *Lord of the Rings* analogy for me really but I try and keep up.

'Ring wraiths are the bad guys right?'

'You bet, scary dudes on horseback with no faces and Darth Vader breath. Well cool. Anyway. I need a favour.'

He tells me no more, just beckons and goes back outside.

'Brother Basil wants a driver, he has an important meeting in Brackton. Now it should be me really, but I don't want to go.' He laughs. 'You see you think you've got discipline problems. Would you do it? Drive the Baz to town? About ten miles away. You get on well with him don't you?' He snaps his fingers. 'Hey! You can ask him about fasting!'

So now I'm sitting in an old Ford Mondeo, learning how the gears work as I drive. Brother Basil is his usual cheery self. So to bring him down a bit I ask about failure.

'We do have a tendency to disappoint ourselves don't we?' he says. 'I do it all the time. But the confusing thing about it is that we set our own agendas. So what we're often failing to do is please ourselves and others. I find that confusing.'

'What do you mean?'

'Well you may decide to do something, say I don't know... fast for a while...'

How does he know that?

'And then you can't do it,' he laughs suddenly, 'I remember a time when I was going to fast for a week. Had it all planned out, God was going to be so pleased with me. I lasted an hour. I ate more than I would if I hadn't been fasting!'

He laughs again. Has he been talking to Brother Ben? I ask him.

'No, why? Anyway. Failure is how we learn. Look at dear old Peter. His time with Jesus is one long series of mishaps. Sinking in water, cutting off the wrong ears, telling Jesus he can't die, denying they were ever friends, worrying about John when he should have been concentrating on himself.' He counts them off on his fingers. 'Look at that – a whole handful! And why? Why all those mistakes? 'Cause he was trying to follow Jesus. Wouldn't have made any of them if he'd stuck to fishing. Life would have been much simpler. But you don't want a simple life do you?'

I think I'd settle for one right now.

'No you don't. You're like Peter and me, bumbling along, tripping over your own feet and putting them in your mouth every so often. Trying to make something out of your life and faith. It's okay. It's the nature of the beast. And...' he wags a finger at me, 'to be honest about that is a wonderful mark of humility.'

'I'm not humble. Not in the way you are.'

'Yes you are! You're much more humble than me.'

And then we somehow move into this strange twilight zone where we argue about whether I am more humble than Brother Basil. Me, a biscuit-stuffing loser verses Brother B, a wise old monk. He won't let me win the argument and I nearly punch his lights out. We agree to differ.

'You see, God loves this sort of thing,' he says.

What sort of thing?

'Humility. Honesty. Muddling along. I'm a terrible ratbag you know. Terrible. But there's no doubt he thinks I'm terrific.'

And that ends the conversation. I drive and he sits there happily.

Day 34: Career Opportunities

'During his time in the wilderness Jesus aligns himself with the hungry, the powerless and the insignificant. He will not feed his face, he will not perform spectacular acts, he will not become a dominant public figure. He sees these as contrary to his mission. Instead he becomes small and broken and empty. The best shape for the road ahead. The world does not need more spectacles and dominance. That would not serve it well at all. It needs something else.'
Up The Creek Having Burnt The Paddle by Pew Hadovood

- - - - - - - - - - -

I lost my job because I lost other things. Energy. Hope. Self-respect. Kept turning up late and forgetting to do things. That isn't the reason on the redundancy slip, but someone had to go and it was looking for a long time as if I wasn't really putting in much of an appearance anyway. My work ethic was in a skip out the back somewhere. So it was me. I went. Me and my own stupidity. My own frustration and angst. The thing is I never thought I'd end up in that job. Working in that kind of company like that, doing this kind of work all day. I had other plans, I'd set my course on another road. How come it ended in that cul-de-sac? For a while I just couldn't see past that. I wanted to be fired. I wanted to have a reason to walk away. And they handed it to me on a plate.

The first thing I did was walk down the road to *Starbucks*. I ordered coffee and sat there in a daze. I had no job and I was relieved. But I also had no job and I was scared. I didn't know what I wanted to do, I didn't know what I could do, I just knew that I couldn't do that anymore. So I sat and drank and stared and from nowhere the idea to revisit Moorfield Monastery crept into my thinking. As I sat there weakly stirring the cold dregs and watching people in suits order confident beverages to accompany their meetings and laptop conferences, I decided I should do it. I should hide. Not have to face this kind of thing anymore. I had been to Moorfield in my early twenties for a weekend. Now I'd go in my forties for a whole bunch of weekends. And the midweeks in between. It was January and I figured that with Lent looming it was the perfect thing to do. You could even call it divinely appointed. So I called and I packed and I came.

And thirty four days later I'm scared again. As I sit in lunch stirring the cold dregs of my leek soup, watching the men in habits go about their well-ordered lives, I fear the worst. That I will return to my flat and do what I did the week before coming to Moorfields. I will lie in bed all day. Not washing, not caring, not hoping. Staring at TV programmes that offer me nothing but better ways to cook a piece of haddock. I put my chin in my hand and realise that I haven't shaved for two days. See? The madness is lurking again.

Perhaps I could become a monk? No, I'm too rebellious. A vicar then? No, I'm not sociable enough, too reclusive. An archaeologist adventurer perhaps, fighting bad guys and globe-trotting for lost treasure? Yep. That's sorted it then. I'll do that. I feel a presence beside me. I turn to look. It's not God, though I'm sure he's around at the moment. No. It's Brother Fin.
    'Tell me if this is no good,' he says in his quiet way. 'But I wondered if you wanted to read this and fill it in?'
He places a tidy pile of papers next to my soup bowl. One corner lands in a perfectly-formed circle of spilt food.
    'Is it an application to be a monk?' I say, but he shakes his head profusely.
    'Not at all. It's one of those job analysis things. I hear you were wondering what to do.'
When? Just now? Was I thinking aloud? Rambling over my leek soup?
    'Brother Ben told me. We just wondered if it might help.'
That Brother Ben. He's the news man round here, no doubt.
I stare at the pile of papers. I have nothing to lose so I take it.

If this was my old life I'd take it down to *Starbucks* and fill it in as I watched the world get caffeinated. But it isn't so instead I wander along to the lake, sit on the grass and work my way through a hundred quickfire questions. They are multiple choice so I'm never stuck for an answer. Just sometimes lost for the right one. It's like *Who wants to be a millionaire* without the audience and the big payout. Takes me the best part of half an hour, and then more time to work out how many a's b's c's and d's I have. And then exactly what thirty seven a's means and twenty three b's etc. I'm guessing professional form-filler will not feature highly on my list. In the end other things come out on top. Looks like I'm going to be Prime Minister then. So that's that solved. I sit by the water for a long time thinking about swimming in it. I'm not planning to go head first in there again but I'm glad I once did. Brother Basil is a crafty guy. For a man trying to keep some kind of control of his life I was recklessly out of whack in that water.

Now here I am with a pile of papers and still no clue about how to get back on the ladder of life. I feel like Mr Small. Unable to stick my head up and get a break. At least Zacchaeus had his tree. I have heard so many success stories on the TV and radio. The problem with these is that no one broadcasts all the other tales. Success stories make better headlines than tales of failure. 'Blessed are the poor,' Jesus said. And, 'Blessed are the poor in spirit.' One means those who have little income. The other refers to those who aren't so spiritual. Looks like I could be doubly blessed then.

Day 35: You've Got A Friend

The pressure is starting to ease. Standing on the temple he would not, could not call the angels. That would have been disastrous. He knows that was some kind of rehearsal for another time. A time when he will be tempted again to do the spectacular and avoid death. But not now. Now the danger has passed. Now it is okay to seek help. And so the two men drop by. He hasn't had company in five weeks, apart from the animals and the devil and his own shadow. Now strangers bring him fresh water. Like Hagar with that angel when she collapsed and left her baby hidden beneath that bush. He never thought he would die in the way that she did, but it is the same figure that rescued her that now sits in the sand and talks with him. A wolf hangs around too, pacing back and forward, scuffing dust and stones with its paws, but there's little real danger with his two visitors there.

- - - - - - - - - - -

It's beginning to hit me. Time is running out. Rather quickly now. When I packed my rucksack and threw myself into my car five weeks ago I was getting away from it all. Now I'm going back to it all. What's changed?

Anything? It was all right for Jesus he had a new career lined up, he was going to strike out and save the world. He had purpose, direction, a game plan. I have nothing more than the carnage I left behind. Admittedly Jesus was also heading for abuse, rejection, torture and death, and I don't envy him that. I'm keen to avoid that kind of job offer. Was he totally aware of the danger ahead when he prepared to move on from the rocks and solitude? He probably took it one day at a time. Which is always a good game plan.

Am I different? Are these lonely days proving something, making me into something? I didn't exactly come looking for a vision. I really just knew I had the time to do something different. When else do you get enough weeks to live out something like this? Mind you if things don't buck up soon, I'll be able to do all this again next month, 'cause the future right now is little more than a yawning chasm. A second-hand canvas hastily recovered so it's ready for another burst of sketches and graffiti.

I feel panicky about it all. There's no doubt about that. The possibilities seem somehow too small and too big. Anything might happen back out there in that massive world. Or nothing. Or worse than nothing. The cinema. I could end up back there, ten years older and still scraping bubblegum and carrying bags of vomit. I need to distract myself. I go down to the quad looking for Brother Ben. Instead I meet Brother Fin. He nods at me. He is kicking a football at the outside wall of the quad. He's pretty good with the footwork, passes it from foot to foot, then to the wall, in the air, off his head a couple of times, then his right knee, left knee, right knee, left knee, onto his chest and through the routine again.

'I think I know why I hated all that number crunching now,' I say, waving the sheaf of papers at him.
He nods. 'Supposed to be a sea captain eh? Or perhaps a lollipop man?'
   'Bingo caller,' I say and I'm not kidding.
   'Really? You're kidding?' He catches the ball.
Like I say, I wasn't.
   'Top three scores, Bingo Caller, TV Presenter or Author.'
Brother Fin spins the ball in his fingers, the black and white merging in a flashing blur of grey.
   'Not a monk then?' he says eventually.
I laugh. 'Not yet. The good thing is... I do see why I was bored and angry in my last job.'
   'Lots of people are bored and angry in their jobs.'
It's Brother Ben.
   'True, but at least I understand why.'
   'Which one are you gonna go for then?' Brother Ben asks. 'Let me guess. Not the Bingo.'
   'Good guess. I think I'll just go down the Jobcentre and look for a job as a successful author.'

'There are lots of ways to write,' says Brother Fin. 'You just have to find your own way of making it work.'
He boots the ball at the wall and it bounces back and smacks Brother Ben in the chest.
'Ow!' he yelps. 'You should go and see Aidan.'
Aidan? For careers advice?
Brother Fin agrees. 'You should go and see Aidan.'

I knock on Brother Aidan's door. I've been back there on and off over the weeks but it's been a while. As ever there is no response. I wait the longest time, longer than ever, but there is nothing. Until I raise my fist to knock a second time and then the usual, 'Come.'
I go in. As usual Brother Aidan seems furious with me until I mention someone, anyone, from fifteen hundred years ago. Then we're back on safe ground. Bad Aidan slips into the wings and Good Aidan is back on stage. We chat about Cuthbert and Wilfred and the like for a short time. Then I hold up a hand and jam a spoke in the wheels.
'It's great hearing about these heroes, but how can these old guys help me now? I don't know what I'm going to do when I leave here. I have no idea. The others told me to come and see you. You know, Brother Ben and Brother Fin.'
'Really?' he says. I say nothing.
The truth is I'm angry, I know I joked about the job survey with the guys but I'm fed up. It's all very well being told you should be a successful author but no one's out there waiting to give you a job. You won't find that little white card advertising the post of *Novel writer. Pen name optional. Fifty grand a year. Only apply if you've done that job survey.* Doesn't happen. Yesterday, after I'd finished the questionnaire, I walked around for a while ranting at the sky. Nothing happened, it didn't solve anything. I just wore myself out. Being out of work is sapping my meaning. My self-confidence is slipping through my fingers. There's the fear that I won't find anything again, and that will mean no money, and no decent way of life. But it'll also mean looking like I wasted everything. Embarrassment and ridicule hang around my door like a couple of drug dealers waiting to do me irreparable damage.

I fully expect Bad Aidan to re-emerge and send me off to wash my mouth out and learn some manners. But instead he looks at me for a long time, chewing on the blackened, battered nail of his little finger. I've not seen him do that before. Eventually he says, 'Did we discuss St Francis? No? A relatively recent saint. Thirteenth century. Founded the Franciscan order of course. You know something? He came to a crisis. Yes he did. He was a wealthy merchant, and a playboy and a soldier. Then he had a vision.'

How do people get these visions? I haven't had a vision.

'It ruined his life,' Brother Aidan says.

Oh well, I don't want one then.

'It broke him and made him. No more wealth or wars or women. It led him into poverty and compassion. Now my guess is you don't want that.'

He nibbles his finger nail again.

'No I don't want that.'

'No, but my guess is you weren't designed for that. You see, I firmly believe that Francis was made to be a poor leader. But he didn't start out that way. It was always inside of him waiting to come out. It just took a vision to open the can. What's your vision?'

And he stops. I wait but there is no more.

I don't know what my vision is. I have no idea what will 'open the can'. And this is not the kind of careers advice I recall from my school days. Highly unorthodox.

Day 36: Wherever I Lay My Hat

A leopard paces where the wolf had been yesterday. The first he knows about it is when he wakes to hear the soft padding sound. He turns his head, careful to make no noise. The big cat slinks from left to right, it has a grace, an air of superiority and confidence. There is no rush, just the restless passing from left to right.

It's so familiar now this place. He could stay. He's happy alone. Used to the hardships. He has made peace with the desert and himself. He would need food but that could be arranged. He could avoid so much by remaining in the desert and becoming a mystic. People could come and visit him for guidance and help. His ministry would grow and develop and word would spread. He could lead by example, throw off the world's pressures and change things from his cave out here in the desert. It could work.

Of course there'd be no final sacrifice. No death to end the system of violence. No great and terrible day when the moon is eclipsed and turns to the colour of blood. There will still be an eclipse and the sky will still grow dark, but it won't signify anything. Joel's prophecy will have been wasted. There may be signs in the sky but the earth will be strangely still. The nails and the wood meant for him will be used on someone else. And there'll be no empty tomb. Because his body will be here in this cave. If he stays in the desert he can serve the world in a different way. Wash the feet of any who come to see him. The poor, the grieving, the persecuted, the humble. But he can't sit down with them in the gutters of Galilee, he can't meet the hopeless in their own dark places. They'll need to come to him. And most significantly, those calling on the name of the Lord won't be saved. Not at all. That piece of Joel's jigsaw will be missing.

So he sits and stares at the leopard. Prowling, staring, menacing. It's moving gradually closer and he can't tell whether it's just curious or hungry. It's not the true enemy though. The true enemy is the desire to give up.

- - - - - - - - - -

I wake early with a headache. Feel a bit sick too. I thought retreats were supposed to be holy, peaceful things. The peace and abandonment I felt the night I ventured out with Ben and Fin seem light years away. Clearly there will be no state of celestial bliss coming my way any time soon. No sign that I'm about to crashland in a zen-like place of enlightenment. Just nausea. I'm not sure that my trip to Brother Aidan helped much, I feel this pressure now to find my 'vision', to somehow get out that crowbar and 'open the can'.

Mostly though, I don't want to go home. I want to stay. I don't even know if I have a home anymore. I mean I have a flat and a fridge and a carpet that needs a darn good hoovering. But they are not my home. Not really. This shed with all its stains and cobwebs and outside toilet has become that. This is where I belong. The walls here and the beams and the trips to the refectory and the chapel. The monks chanting, the smell of lunch soup, the chatting with Brothers Ben and Basil. These are my world now. To leave them could be disastrous, would just plunge me back into chaos and anarchy. There is order here, huge meaning in the small things. So I decide. I'm going to stay another month. That's the way forward. Another four weeks and I'll have my vision. Thirty days and my can will be well and truly opened. I go down to see Brother Wilfred in the office.

It's strange to see a man in a habit sitting behind a computer. Two worlds colliding. Brother Wilfred looks like an astute man. He is, after all, the brother who runs the business. He listens carefully to my well-reasoned argument. He nods a lot, he pushes his steel-rimmed glasses back up his nose a few times with a finger covered in ink. He is sympathetic, a patient man used to listening. He nods some more.
    'I see, yes I see,' he says, a little nervously. 'That sounds good. Yes, very good.'
So I can stay?
    'The thing is… we're booked up.'

And that's it. I can't pursue my Godly vision because other people want a holiday. Great. I limp back, it had seemed such a watertight idea. I hadn't bargained on other people needing some time out. Don't they know I'm on a mission here, do they care nothing for my long-term welfare?

So that's that. I can't stay. I can't hang around in the wings of my own life. Have to go out and face the crowd with all their unreasonable demands and attitudes.

Day 37: Dreams

'Forty days is still a long time. A long, long time. We easily read it, and it's gone in a few verses. But doing this small project of trying to come up with a pocket book of soundbite wisdom has made me realise just how long this period is. Faith is often seen as an adventure, an exciting journey, but much of the Bible deals with the opposite – the gradual unravelling of our days. Most of us have lives of waiting, lives of hoping for something better. Joseph (he of the multi-coloured coat) spent years in prison, Abraham and Moses both spent years wandering in the wilderness, Ruth's whole life was ordinary, except for the extreme poverty she and Naomi experienced, Jesus lived three decades that were so normal they barely get a mention in the Bible. To hope for something better is to subject ourselves to years of trusting, believing, crying out for something more. So this reflection is for you if your life feels mundane at times, and you long for more...'
Up The Creek Having Burnt The Paddle by Pew Hadovood

- - - - - - - - - - -

He stirs in his sleep, sits up suddenly, blinking into the night. Stars flash at him. The cold night presses on his body. Was that a dream or is someone else really here? Moses and Elijah. He was talking with them. About death and glory. He claws at the immediate memory of it. Jerusalem, they were talking about that holy city, soon to be a place of endings and new starts. Moses and Elijah? Were they here in the desert? Or was he dreaming? He stands, walks around, stretches his cold limbs. He even calls out. 'Hello?'
Nothing.

He wishes they were there, company now would be good. He hunches again, sits and pulls his knees to his chest. A footstep, but not a friend. A hyena pads towards him. It stops a few steps away, twists its head as it studies him. One day children and hyenas will play together. Jackals and scorpions will be household companions. But not yet. Not until his discussion with Moses and Elijah has borne fruit. Not for a long time yet. The hyena stares, eyes like perverse jewels. He picks up a rock and throws it past the animal. It bucks, flinches, backs away. He looks to the sky and prays aloud. The sudden sound of his voice pushes the animal further away. Dark figures step out of the night towards him but it's not Elijah and Moses. These are other friends, come to sit with him in the dark.

- - - - - - - - - - -

I dream about my grandfather. A strong, upright man who always smoked a pipe and had a cupboard in the corner by his chair, full of gadgets and tools and magical things from a hundred years back. I loved that cupboard and I loved my granddad. We would play and talk and laugh and I thought that men like him went on forever. Then one day he was lying in a bed and people told me he wouldn't be around much longer. He looked a different man, as if someone had taken granddad's face, sucked life out of it and placed it on a smaller person. He lay in that bed for a week and I watched him move from one world to another, the memories playing in my mind like a movie trailer. Fast flickering images summing up a lifetime in a few minutes. I watched him go and I replayed those memories in my head again and again and again. In my dream he is alive again and well and we are the double act we once were. He teaches me new things and I laugh a lot. I have no idea how old I am, or how old he is. It is timeless and it doesn't matter. What matters is that for a few brief moments he is alive again and we are together. I wake with my eyes leaking tears. I don't want the dream to fade, I lie as still as possible clinging onto every image of it, every moment of old feeling that it brought back. I play the scenes again, rewinding and fast-forwarding them. But it's no good, the more I try and cling on the quicker the experience slips away. Granddad melts back into the shadows. Returns to his world, leaving me in mine. I think on others who have gone there. Friends. Family. This world seems so real, so immediate, so all-important. But it's not long before time is up and the credits are rolling.

I find Brother Basil, as ever, surrounded by chickens in his Armageddon of a garden. For some reason he's cleaning up a chunk of rock which looks for all the world like the philosopher's stone. I tell him about my dream. He thinks for a while.

'It's probably about endings,' he says. 'Initially your time in the cabin, but other things too. Your days are drawing to a close here, which is most likely stirring up other things in you. I wonder if you'd do something for me.'

He bends and picks up a stone from his garden. There is nothing significant about it, could be one of a hundred lying about here. He hands it to me.

'If you can, take this and throw it into the lake, that one we swam in the other night. Let it represent where you are now and all that's happened. Your wife, the baby, your job.'

I go to speak but he holds up a hand.

'I'm not asking you to throw all that away, it's not about that, and I'm not saying this will solve anything. It's an action that's all. If you do this then you will always know that one day in your time here you let go. With what little energy you had. As much as you were able you handed over those things to God. You'll have that memory and I'll know it too. Sometimes a physical activity can facilitate the soul, help express things when the words are missing. Just go to the lake, pray something, anything, and throw this rock. Will you do that for me?'

I do it. I make sure no one else is around to see me. I look to the sky and stumble over some words about the people I've lost, including granddad. It feels hollow and inadequate but it makes me cry. I pass the stone between my hands, twist it in my fingers, throw it up in the air and catch it a few times. It suddenly seems a big thing I'm doing. I think on the dream again, let granddad's memory warm and break my heart a little. Then suddenly, unexpectedly, I sling the rock, a crumb of Brother Basil's garden. It doesn't go far, I've never been a great thrower. Not good at getting stones skimming over water. It splashes and sinks and no one else is there to witness it. I feel nothing. I stand and stare at the lake for a long time. The ripples are quickly gone, and then I'm staring at calm water.

Day 38: Every Day I Write the Book

He writes in the dust again. His finger racing like a desert bug fleeing for its life. His hand twists this way and that, leaving trails that form the kind of pictures and stories that will last forever. He pauses abruptly as a moment of vision distracts him, he glances up and sees a woman lying in the same dust just beyond his creation, her clothes torn and her face scuffed and spattered. When he looks up a second time she has gone. But he will remember that face, and one day he may well write in the dust again, and create a new life for her.

He is writing of the first creation again, bringing the world into being for a second time. Light, space, liquid, matter, growth, order, creativity, purpose, colour. He tells the story again in these hastily drawn figures. The dawn of time, sitting outside of time. Existing before the clocks began ticking. The whole of history looking like one large canvas to him. The past here, the future there, the present all over it. Nothing linear, but a sprawling epic in a single telling. A picture and a million words.

Before too long he will tell the creation story a third time. Not spoken or written in the dust then, but with his living and dying and living again. The new creation. The new beginning. He will walk into the dark and disappear, and three days later there will be light. And he will re-emerge into a new world, a world where everything is different. Though it may still look the same. A matrix reformed. An invisible kingdom seeping its way quietly into the old order. The spider's web breached. The net torn. The controlling hands with their fingers now dislocated. Let there be light, and there will be light. The light of the world. Not a city on a hill, but a cross. A beacon no one can put out. The light that leads to life. He draws again. Three crosses appear. He catches his breath. Dusts his hands and stands. Enough drawing for now.

- - - - - - - - - -

The library! Why did I not find this place before? Why does life do this? Just when time is running out I find the Holy Grail. The Eldorado for bookworms. A page-turner's Shangri-la. A vast, epic room stacked with ancient reads of all shapes and sizes. Brown, gold, cream, tan... the dust jackets are everywhere, some of them as big as my head. And the other end of the scale too. Tiny, hardbacked pocket books. Classics from years gone by, handled and mishandled and passed on and snuck in jacket pockets from decade to decade. There's a colossal religious section of course, everything from St Paul's favourite finger food to Pope Madagascar the third's nasal grooming habits. But that's just one wall, there are three others jammed with fiction, travel, philosophy, biography, comedy... wow! There's a huge comedy section. Monks either laugh a lot or need to laugh a lot.

I spend forever pulling books off shelves and laying them open on a table that's about the size of the Serengeti. I jump from book to book, reading random pages, flicking back and forward, studying flyleaves and cover notes. I won't remember much of anything but it's not about that. It's about being here in this ancient room. The afternoon sun blasting its way through the dust and the smears on the window, lighting up this place of learning and entertainment. It's about the atmosphere and mystery created by a roomful of characters and their claims. For a long time I channel-hop from read to read, then I find a glorious old copy of Danton Haynes's *Dreams and Fiction* and I press myself into a huge armchair and lose myself in his tale of murder and fabrication.

I shiver. The book is a little macabre and the light is going. The library now feels more like the kind of place where a bunch of monks might gather to discover who the murderer is. I catch sight of *The Name of The Rose* on a nearby shelf and I can only think of Sean Connery and the inquisition. I read on. I jump chapters because I read half of it ten years ago and want to get to the end this time. Haynes's style is fast, he writes in gripping, clipped sentences. This happens. Then this. Then that.

Daniel is a tough but compassionate guy. He doesn't mess around. He solves dark problems with his mate Hugo. He's a modern day

Wilberforce crossed with Indiana Jones. But that's not the primary tale here. Daniel frees slaves and rescues kidnap victims, but it's Martine who takes centre stage. When the book opens she is in the nursery. Staring at their cot. There is a knock at the door, but she doesn't hear it. Her mind is on the baby. Daniel goes to the door, he's a little worse the wear for drink. It's Nate at the door. A friend from school days. Just what Daniel needs right now, a soul mate. They sit. They chat. The drinks flow. Nate has come a long way, he is bronzed from a month in Asia, working with his own company out there. But he came back when he got the news that things were not well with Daniel. Nate is an intuitive guy, he gets hunches, sees things other people don't see. He got a hunch about Daniel, phoned up his old mate. Jumped on a plane to come and sit with him and share a drink or two. Daniel needs this now, he comes clean. It's the mother of all messes. Hugo is dead. A tragedy on a mission. It's unthinkable. He was so full of life. Daniel breaks down. Nate tries to comfort him but it's no good. Daniel won't be comforted. His mate Hugo is gone. They were together through thick and thin. What happened? Simple. They took time out last summer, spent time together in a castle in Spain. Castles have plenty of lost and lonely corners. Places to drink wine and study the view. That's where Daniel seduced Martine. She fought it but he was in up to his neck. Had watched her swim and sunbathe and hang around in too few clothes. Hugo was oblivious, out exploring here, there and everywhere, diving, climbing, caving. Meanwhile Daniel and Martine drank wine and looked at the view. And Daniel grew increasingly obsessed. One problem. Hugo and Martine were husband and wife. So Daniel hatched a plan. Just one night's pleasure. Just one time together and no one would know. Fine. But events took their course and poor Martine found herself cornered. Ambushed by circumstances. She had never wanted this with him, fought it every step of the way, and now she was paying the price. She told him the news late one night when Hugo was asleep. In one of those dark and distant rooms where they had made love. She is pregnant. And there is no way Hugo is involved. The world collapses in on him. He panics. He cannot face his best friend with this. So they hatch a plan. He crumbles but she digs deep and finds strength. He will go away for a week and during that time she will make damn sure she has sex with her husband. So Daniel disappears. Then comes back again. Martine is distraught. Nothing has happened, Hugo seems totally disinterested. Perhaps he guesses something. So Daniel plots and sells his soul to hatch his next miserable plan. He sends his best mate on a mission he knows is doomed to fail. It doesn't take long. Within a week Hugo is missing presumed dead. Another week and there is no presumed about it. He is over. Their friendship is history. The problem is solved. Martine grieves inconsolably, her heart is broken. And all the time she grows bigger. And then the baby is born.

Next door she leans on the cot and lets her mind run over the last few months. Nate pours them both another drink. Daniel talks on. He has ruined all their lives. Hugo. Martine. The baby. There is no way back. He is living in a grey blur. Barely able to get up each day. Nate raises his hand. He has news. Daniel needs to listen up. This is not the first time this story has played out. It has happened before. He has seen it. He knows Martine of old. He knows her from college. She played this game before. What game? There is no game. Daniel shakes his head. But Nate insists. There is. She has broken hearts before, grown bored with her men. Discarded them. Daniel refuses to believe this. She would not have tricked him like this. Why? Why would she? She is not like that. It's all his fault. She tried to stop it, she tried to hold him at bay but it was all him. He was too pushy.

Martine hears Daniel's voice rise and realises he is not alone. She listens, can just catch Nate's voice. She walks to the door and strains to hear. Looks back at the cot. Nate is wiser than Daniel knows. She had watched Daniel for a while, been aware that he was winnable. She has a knack for that sort of thing. So she wooed him. For the challenge of it. Put herself in the right place at the right time. Wore less clothes, brushed against him, brandished the right smile. And when they were alone, she put up just enough fight to make it seem his fault. But it wasn't. It was her game and she was winning it. She was tired of Hugo. Faithful, reliable Hugo. She wanted Daniel now. And more than that, she wanted Daniel's baby. Hugo might have been a great adventurer and a loyal friend, but he was no lover and even worse as a potential father.

Month after month, and no baby in sight. One night with Daniel and there it was.

She walks back to the cot. Strokes the wood again. Once she was pregnant the only problem then was her husband. What to do about dear Hugo? So when Daniel went away she made sure she avoided him. Sleep with him now? She could barely stand to be in the same room. And when Daniel returned she sowed the seed. The idea of sending Hugo somewhere dangerous. Goodbye Hugo. Hello Daniel. Perfect.

Until this.

Daniel's eyes are wet, he cannot believe what he is hearing. He cannot believe he is hearing Nate use the words scheming and Martine in the same sentence. His life is turning into hell.
Back in the nursery she sighs and stands. No point staying here. No point dreaming now.
The baby is gone. Lost before it had really started to grow. The cot is empty. She flips off the light, puts on her best smile and opens the door. She pauses for a second, framed there. Nate is not bad looking. She gives him her best smile. He may believe he knows her, but men never know as much as they think. He only knows she seduced Daniel. He has no idea she sent Hugo to his death. Maybe he can give her a baby. Hello Nate…

It's dark. The light has gone. The library is awash with shadows and early moonlight. I've missed the meal and at least one service in the chapel.
     'Good book?'
I leap out of my skin. There is a small, thin figure sitting in a chair at the darkest end of the library.
     'Er… yes… very good. Sorry… you scared me.'
Who is this?
     'Love is powerful isn't it? It takes you where you don't want to go.'
He speaks carefully, precisely, his words are framed neatly. 'And I'm

not just talking about romantic love. Sacrificial love too. To love anything is to risk losing it.'

'Yes, but she's mad.'

'I'm not talking about Martine.'

How does he know what I'm reading?

'Without love we can build our walls and fortresses and be self-sufficient. Without love we can construct our castles and make them places where we rule. To begin loving means lowering the drawbridge. Leaving the door open. Allowing the heart and soul to be breached once again. Which... I think you will do.'

The figure stands and moves towards the door. Without much light I still cannot make him out. The door opens and he is gone. I shiver. Who was that? Brother Horace? I can't recall whether there were any yellow socks or not.

Day 39: When You're Young

'One of the fundamental things about Jesus going into the wilderness is that he is taking the glory of God into an unexpected place. A dry, empty, godless desert. A place where wild animals and the devil can roam freely. This is the start of something big – from now on you will not need to go to a 'holy' place to meet God, he will be out there in the gutters and the streets, at the parties and the pagan places. And in the deserts of life. It has happened a few times in the Old Testament days – Naaman getting healed in the Jordan, God showing up in a strange, pagan land to Ezekiel when the people had been kidnapped by a godless nation, and again in the terrible city of Nineveh. But now it is starting big time. Now you can bump into God anywhere. In three years the temple curtain will be shredded, opening up access to everyone. And Jesus is already demonstrating that reality now. When John begins his writings about the life of Jesus he starts with an unexpected phrase. He says – 'We have seen the glory of God!' Yes they have – and unlike some of those Old Testament folk – they lived! They didn't die! They in fact felt better – not worse. The glory of God is now accessible – to be found with sweat on his brow, a smile on his lips, telling stories and upsetting the status quo... experiencing the pain and disorder of this damaged world.'
Up The Creek Having Burnt The Paddle by Pew Hadovood

- - - - - - - - - - -

Then Jesus, full of the Holy Spirit, left the Jordan River. He was upbeat, inspired, spurred on by his cousin's bold pronouncements about him. And so he walked away from the river, and the distracting rumble of the crowd. Into silence, towards the heat and the creatures of the desert. And vulnerability. His only companion the spirit of God, silent, unafraid, present but not apparent. And the days ticked by slowly. Unravelling to the sound of his grumbling stomach. And after many long, lonely nights filled with dreams and visions, the Devil came and tempted him. Then the Devil said to him, 'If you are the Son of God, form a woman from this dust. The way you did in the beginning. It's not good for a man to be alone.'

Jesus scooped up a handful of sand and weighed it in his fingers. He recalled those moments when the earth transformed into the beautiful shape of a human being for the first time.

'Think of all those women you have seen, you could have any of them. Couldn't one of them keep you warm in the desert night?'

He looked up and said, 'No! The scriptures say, "Can a man heap fire into his lap and not be burned? Can he walk on hot coals and not blister his feet?"'

And he let the soft mound of sand slip away to nothing.

Then the Devil took him up and revealed to him all the comforts of the world. The Devil told him, 'I will give you the glory of complete access to all of these – personal freedom, success and satisfaction any time you like. They are mine to give, yours to take. And you can have them if you will just bow down and worship me.'

Jesus considered the offer and replied, 'If I accept these I will be bowing down to you by doing just that. The scriptures say, "It is better to give than to receive." True nourishment comes from kindness and compassion, not from self-satisfaction. Not from greed or lust. "Your care for others is the measure of your greatness."'

So the Devil took him to Jerusalem, to the highest point of the Temple, and pointed down towards the oppressed people below. He said, 'If you are the Son of God sort out the world's problems! You can see the great need here. Be a saviour for the people, get rid of all their troubles. For the Scriptures say, "There will be no more crying or pain, and God will wipe away every tear from their eyes." You can do it! Snap your fingers. Now. Stop hanging around.'

Jesus responded, 'In this world there is trouble. I have overcome the world, but love, not power, is the way of God. The scriptures say, "Worship the Lord your God with all your heart, mind, will and strength, serve only him."'

'You talk of love,' said the Devil, 'but if you love people you will give them a better life. Come on! Reveal yourself to the world. Stop hiding, stop being invisible and silent. People think you are unjust. They say you have forgotten them. They say you don't exist, that you are simply a product of the imagination.'

'My time has not yet come. And you do not understand the one who sent me. People will see the son of man sitting at God's right hand and coming in glory. But not yet. That time is not here. And the scriptures also say, "Do not test the Lord your God."'

When the Devil had finished tempting Jesus, he left him, waiting for the next opportunity to arise. Jesus walked back to his cave, exhausted.

Now there is only one day left. He crawls inside the opening in the rock, into the cool and the dark. It will be good to eat again. He curls up and hides from the world. Tomorrow he will be with friends. He will miss the desert, but he is ready to leave the loneliness behind. It has not been easy to keep perspective in this place where the devil roams a little too freely. Without others around he has battled to keep his thoughts in check. Others have ventured into deserts and begged to die, Elijah, Job, David. But he has come through. He has faced himself and the emptiness and come out the other side.

- - - - - - - - - -

A soon as I wake I feel the panic rise in me again. Only one day left and still no real plan for the future. I wash in cold water in my little sink, the bar of soap is almost worn to nothing. I dry my face and dress and push the terror away, after all, there's a whole day left. I wonder about revisiting the library. There's a shiver on my spine as I remember the stranger I met. Perhaps I won't go back.

I find myself wondering what Jesus did on day 39. Knowing that the following morning it would all end. Was he tempted to finish early? Cut it a day short and slip back to Nazareth for a nap in bed? It's the last mile which can be the hardest, the last hour, the last minutes of the waiting. Perhaps he started making lists in the sand, things he needed to do. And was there another prophet waiting in the wings? Another young man about to start his desert experience. Was his cave booked up for the next forty days? Did he leave any message scrawled on the wall?

A knock on my door, a couple of raps, the sound is keen, enthusiastic. I open it. There's a sandy-haired guy, blue eyes and freckles, looks about fifteen. He holds out his hand.

'Hi I'm Karl,' he says. 'I'm the next tenant!'

I tell him he's a day early and he laughs.

'I'm in the big house till tomorrow. I take up where you leave off.'

He sticks his head in the shed, looks around at the beams and the furniture.

'This'll do,' he says chirpily.

This'll do? This'll do? What's wrong with the place? He points towards the kettle, he doesn't need to say more, I put it on. He waves his own mug at me. It has Simon Cowell's face on it.

'I hear you have biscuits too,' he says.

'Actually I do this kind of communion thing.'

'I know.'

How? Oh yes – Brother Ben has told him.

'You like The Giggheads too,' he says.

I make the tea and fish out my final packet of Bourbon biscuits.

He bows his head. I consider this then decide to say a little prayer. It becomes a big prayer. About my time past and his time coming. I get so carried away I almost forget to say thanks for the tea and biscuits and what it represents. Eventually Karl looks up.

'Thanks,' he says. 'That was cool.'

'Why are you here?' I ask. 'I mean why are you spending time in a monastery?'

'Don't tell anyone but I'm thinking about becoming a monk.'

Seriously?

'Don't you want to do anything else first?' I ask.

'Like what?'

'Girls? Fast cars? Partying?'

'I've done plenty of that already,' he says. 'Now it's time to do the God thing.'

'I don't think it's just one of those things you can try for a while and then tick off your "to do" list.'

'I know that.'

'You're not running away from anything are you?'
Ah. Wasn't meant to be a searching question, I was only making conversation. But clearly, just for a second, there seems to be a nail and I seem to have hit it. He shakes his head.

'Course not. Wanna be a monk.'
I tell him to chat to Ben and Basil. I figure between the two of them they'll know what to say to Karl. Most likely the same advice from opposite corners.

After he's gone to search out the library I go for a walk to ponder his invasion. How can he be moving into my shack? That's not fair. It's mine. My shed! My bed will still be warm when he throws his bag on it and makes tea in his Simon Cowell mug. How can life move on so rapidly? It feels like a bar of soap sometimes, you grab it and it shoots from your fingers. No holding onto it. So unfair. Just when you think you have it. I recall the days when it's been misty, that rampant, uncontainable cloud that engulfs everything. The ungrippable God. The box-breaker deity. Life moves on and God moves on. Not really a lot of point hanging around in an old draughty shed if the cloud has moved on. At least that's what I tell myself.

I end up breaking bread twice. Probably not kosher but I don't think the God of Brother Basil and Brother Ben will mind. The God of Brother Aidan maybe. But Aidan isn't there. Just Ben and Basil. They both drop by in the afternoon, independently coming to see me and merging their visit. More tea and there's still two thirds of the Bourbons left.

'You made it,' says Ben.
We raise our various mugs and cups.
'Yea, I'm not sure where I've ended up,' I say.
'Same place as most of us,' says Brother Basil, 'on the road again. Heading somewhere.'
'Reminds me of *Nowhere Fast*,' says Ben, pointing at the mp3 player. 'Track seven.'

'I was thinking that,' I say, 'it's a good one for me right now. "Limping along, pumping this song in my ears, wonder how long I'll be limping along through these years."'
Brother Basil's face becomes suddenly serious.

'I've been thinking. I wonder whether you should consider becoming a monk.'
He doesn't smile and my life flashes before my eyes. All those services. All that soup.
But Ben can't hold it. His face cracks and he splutters and laughs. Brother Basil shakes his head.

'Young Ben,' he said. 'You disappoint me.'

'So... not a monk?' I venture, hope creeping into my voice.
Now they both laugh.

'Not unless you heard the call,' says Brother Ben. 'Hey! Maybe God is speaking to you through The Giggheads – you know, track four.'
Track four?

'Mmm... could be.'
Brother Basil nods too, which is worrying. Does he know The Giggheads? Track four on *Long John Silver's Missing Leg*? I can't remember it, why can't I remember it?
We chat about other things, but my mind is distracted now. Trying to work out which track God might be speaking to me through.

When they've gone I hastily flick to track four. *It's Like I'm In A Movie.* That's weird, it's all about a guy who invents a dream machine, a little silver box which sits beside his bed and records his dreams. It's extra useful as it also doubles as an alarm clock. Each morning when he wakes up, and can only remember parts of his dreams, he can play them back on the dream machine and watch the whole thing. So what's that got to do with anything? Other than if I invented the machine I could make my living from selling it.

I listen to it repeatedly. Three, four, five times. Over and over and over. What is it? What does Ben mean? How can my future be in this song? The dreams in track four play out like an action movie and the guy looks like James Bond, winning battles and overcoming bad guys. There is a lot of chasing and escaping death by the narrowest margin. At the end of the song the guy harnesses his dreams and makes them all come true. And he is disappointed. He doesn't want his dreams to come true, he wants to go on dreaming them. But he didn't know that. Makes me realise I don't even have any dreams. I don't know what I'd make come true if I could, I'm aiming at that old target called nothing. And I'm most likely going to hit it.

I catch Brother Ben later at the end of evening chapel.

'I got your meaning about track four,' I whisper. (We have to whisper, we're not supposed to talk after night prayer in the chapel.)

He nods, grins and then says, 'What meaning?'

'You know – track four – my dreams.'

'Oh!' his face displays a light bulb moment, 'is that what track four is about? The dream machine? Cool.'

And he goes, nodding as he walks.

Hang on? Does that mean Ben didn't know what track four was about? So was he just joking? Or guessing? Or maybe God inspired him to say that? Which? Which is it? On my last night I go to bed confused, and dream about being chased and fighting bad guys. And they all look like Brother Ben.

Day 40: Moving Out

'Be careful when you emerge from that wilderness, it may have seemed hell on earth at times, you may have hated every moment, but you may also miss its wild places, its rugged lessons, the isolation and the space to be as mad as you truly are. Don't fear the monsters which have emerged during your time there, they are part of you, and rather than taming them or caging them, train them a little, so you can make use of them on some days in the future. And remember, once you have been in the desert you will take part of it with you, wherever you go. Your pockets will always be lined with a few grains of that sand.'
Up The Creek Having Burnt The Paddle by Pew Hadovood

- - - - - - - - - - -

He wakes to the final day and the first day. It's over. He is coming out. Coming out of the desert, coming out of his life as carpenter. He walks, blinking in the light of a new day. He hears the distant voices. Louder, a little louder. He hasn't heard voices like that in a long while. Passes a scorpion. Passes a shadowy figure near a rock.
Passes a distant hyena and a huge mound of rocky bread. Further on there's an intricate tapestry sketched in the dirt, a collection of ideas for all the stories he may tell. He squats down, traces a few of them with his finger then flattens his palm and dusts the picture away. The ideas are in his head now, they've left the ground and will soon become reality. He stands and walks on. The land is littered with the remnants of so many visions and temptations. A good fist of memories left behind.

He walks on. The voices grow louder. Life is looming large. Solitude will soon be that place he can only visit from time to time. The luxury of this kind of extended stay is gone now. It hurt. It hurt him a lot. But only in the way that intense training can hurt, and the muscles of his resolve are well developed now. Time to discover what his learning will look like in public.

He walks on.

No more wilderness. No more desert.

He is gone.

- - - - - - - - - - -

I've not seen any visions. I've not been blinded by any lights on the paths I've walked. No black woman has shown up in my shed to make breakfast for me. I've heard no booming voice from the sky. Instead I have had Brother Basil, Brother Ben, Brother Aidan and Brother Fin. Mitch Levine and Phat Phingers Franklin. Tosh, Stew, Steve & Bill. Doug. And finally Karl.

I could never prove anything, or demonstrate it scientifically, but today I am sure of something and I'm shocked by the realisation. I have met God here. Now, on the day I leave, I feel sure it's happened. More than feeling it, there is something in my mind and strength and will that tells me it has happened. When and how is hard to say. But at last I seem to know it. I don't mean that all my troubles have melted away, far from it, in some ways I'm more aware of them. But I feel a kind of hope. That there will be a way through, a way to work it out. I take a pen and write it large in the back of Brother Aidan's battered brown notebook. I don't want to forget this. I want to mark it for the future, for all those times when I will question it. I date my scribbling and underline it three times.

I lay out my few things on the bed. The meagre clothes, the e-reader, the black leather Bible. Aidan's battered brown notebook. And Ben's mp3 player. I will see him soon and return The Giggheads to him.

Jesus had no fond farewells of course, he said goodbye to no one. I doubt that he and the devil shook hands and gave each other a manly nod. In fact, it seems to have been more a case of the bad guy slipping away into the shadows to plot his next temptations and ordeals for the man from Nazareth. Next time he'd come at Jesus more subtly, through his friends, his family, his mum. Every day. Through the very people he was trying to help.

Jesus had no bag, I guess, no rucksack or Bourbon biscuits. Maybe he took one last long look at those rocks and looked forward to the day when he'd feed a massive crowd. Then he headed for civilisation. A changed man. Weaker and stronger. A determined, lonely servant.

Brother Basil's cottage is empty, but I find him round the back, forking compost into a pile.

'Spring's coming,' he says, 'lots of things to grow. How about you?'

Me?

'Yea, ready to grow some new things?'

I honestly don't know. I tell him I feel different but I'm not entirely sure what that means.

'Well, time will tell. Wait and see what seeds start popping up. Don't rush it.'

Brother Basil must have seen thousands of pilgrims come through this place in his time, I guess I'm just another one. He puts a hand on my arm.

'Thank you,' he says.

For what?

'Thank you for being honest with me. Helps me to be honest.'

And that's it. No long speeches. Not even any kind of male-bonding embrace. A wave of the hand, a smile and he's back to his work. I pass Brother Aidan in the quad. I thank him for his history lessons on the great saints. He nods. Doesn't smile. That's that then.

I walk away. Then I feel a tap on the shoulder. I turn. He's looking at me as if I woke him at four in the morning again.

'Look, I'm sorry about that time with the shower...'

'Quiet,' he says and he studies my face. 'I wasn't sure about this,' he says, 'but I think so now.'

'You think what?'

He hands me a box. Bigger than a matchbox, smaller than an egg box. I look at it.

'What's in it?'

'I don't know. But I want you to keep it.'

'Why?'

He looks down for a long time.

'Because it was given to me when I became a monk by a very wise and godly man. It is God's possibilities for you.'

'Do I open it?'

Wrong question. Brother Aidan frowns at me. Fiercely. Way more than a frown really, it borders on intent.

'Never,' he says. 'To get what is inside you must just keep travelling with the box. Once you open it, once you look at it, you will dismiss it. It'll be gone. And you'll never conquer that world or climb that mountain or create that piece of life.'

Aidan looks so much younger suddenly, as if he's going back in time.

'Resist the temptation to have it all known. Go into the future with the unseen. Let it be what it is.'

He stops.

'Why are you giving this to me, it's like the notebook, it's too precious.'

He doesn't bother to answer. He's looking older again.

'It's yours,' he says.

Brother Ben is in the kitchen, cleaning things. He looks up as I hold out my hand, the mp3 player cradled in it. He shakes his head and grins. 'Keep it,' he says, 'it's a gift. Remember? Promise you'll listen to The Giggheads for ten minutes every day.'

He laughs at his own joke and Brother Fin comes in then, mop in hand. He gives me the quickest of nods.

'Hey want to be a monk for five minutes?' Brother Ben asks and he grabs the mop and shoves it at me. So I finish my time in the monastery cleaning the kitchen floor with the others. Five minutes turns into half an hour and we chat about music and movies and plenty of things I never thought I'd tell a couple of monks. Eventually the time is gone though, they have to go to chapel and I have to go home. I hand him my last half pack of Bourbons. We shake hands and go. I will miss Brother Ben. I will miss him very much.

So I'm going. With Brother Ben's mp3 and Brother Aidan's cardboard box. I'm scared. I have no idea what is around the corner. I don't want the fame Jesus found, and I don't want the crucifixion either. I stroll away from the kitchen, not wanting to leave too quickly. Past the refectory, out of the quad, past Brother Basil's cottage and his chickens, and then further on past my shed. I dawdle near the lake I swam in a hundred years ago with Brother Basil, then on to the car park. A stark reminder of civilisation. Past Brother Basil's Ford Mondeo and onto my own car. The rucksack in the back. The key in the ignition. The engine starting. Handbrake off. Reversing out of the space, then forward towards the lane. I glance back as I pull into the road. That's that then.

I'm gone.

Made in the USA
Lexington, KY
03 July 2018